A CULT OF ONE

A CULT OF ONE

HOW TO DEPROGRAM YOURSELF FROM NARCISSISTIC ABUSE

RICHARD GRANNON

GRANNON
PUBLISHING

A CULT OF ONE
How to Deprogram Yourself from Narcissistic Abuse

FIRST EDITION

ISBN   978-1-5445-3355-1 *Hardcover*
        978-1-5445-3356-8 *Paperback*
        978-1-5445-3354-4 *Ebook*
        978-1-5445-3357-5 *Audiobook*

CONTENTS

CHAPTER 1

THE FIGHT OF MY LIFE

BY THE TIME THE SECOND PUNCH HIT ME IN THE JAW, I SENSED, even through my drunken stupor, that my face was actually taking on damage. Despite the alcohol, it occurred to me that a speedy response on my part would be required to allay further injury. I used a Thai clinch to my opponent's neck and drew him into my shoulder to smother the surprisingly heavy hooks he was landing.

That stopped the punches that, though I did not yet know it, had permanently dislocated my jaw. We wrestled a little. I couldn't see him because he was so close, and my world was momentarily a claustrophobic, dark space of panting breath, grunts, and the sound of our shoes scuffing the floor as we battled for a dominant position.

I released the clinch, and he took the bait. He drew back his meaty fist to hit me again. I saw the opportunity, and I caught him squarely in the nose with a pretty solid headbutt, sending blood squirting down his T-shirt.

My opponent was a solidly built Greek man, squat and girthy. He had clearly trained—as his jaw-breaking punches had shown me—and beneath his fat was real strength. He went in with an upper-body clinch to prevent further skull-to-nose contact, and as he wound me into an "over-under" clinch, I felt the fear that something terrible might befall me.

I responded with a jumping guard. This is a move from Brazilian Jiu Jitsu where you hold the opponent in a clinch and jump up, wrapping your legs around his torso and dragging him to the ground. You end up on your back. This sounds disadvantageous, I know, but, if you know your submissions, it's a potentially good strategy. The trick is that you must be comfortable delivering armbars or triangle chokes. Let me say this: it's fine in competition, and it works great on a safe, matted surface in the gym. However, I would not recommend doing it on a tarmac footpath as I did that evening.

My spine and the back of my head clonked onto the hard path, and my body loudly announced that I had done something both stupid and injurious to my person. I pulled him into a deep closed guard to keep him from using those sheep-shearing Greek farmer's fists on my face any further.

My jaw was dislocated, and my left eye was rapidly closing up. I was prepared to triangle choke or armbar him when he inevitably "posted up," meaning he tried to push away and get upright with his arms. He was ready to go on punching my face into oblivion.

Luckily, the now dreaded farmer's fists of ancient Sparta never landed. As if by some far-off signal heard only by the two of us, locked in that intimate embrace, we simply stopped.

It was over. Our bodies agreed. I unlocked my position, and we both stood up and looked at each other, a little bewildered. His nose was mashed. My face was blowing up like a pumpkin.

The skirmish was brief and violent, and left us both a little shocked, I think. We staggered away from each other perhaps with a little more respect for the other than at the initiation of the event. He left holding his newly reconfigured nose and me my mashed mandible.

This was a fight that I got into at York University at 2:00 a.m. after six solid hours of drinking. It was one of many I mysteriously found myself in as a twenty-something.

I only fought when I could see that a friend was in real danger. The problem was that I had idiotic and reckless friends: privileged kids in private school who enjoyed the adrenaline rush of a brawl. They got away with a few bumps and scrapes. I, on the other hand, had an eye that was completely closed for three days, and my bite is still not aligned properly two decades later. Bearing the burden of other people's poor decisions—cheerfully—is something of a theme in my life.

At age twenty-one, as a devout martial arts enthusiast, I had a penchant for getting into fights with the kind of delusional confidence in my own indestructibility, which is only afforded to those young enough to know no better. I had not internalised truths that I now consider to be self-evident.

For example: there are bigger, tougher, nastier people out there. Even if you beat them, they will come to your house. If you're not in, they will deliver their vengeance to whomever is.

Or even if you "win," the bigger your "win," the more jail time you can get and the nastier the prison you can end up in.

Or simply: I really, really, really don't want to go to prison. Ever. No, not even for fraud in Denmark in one of their famous, luxury five-star jails.

And most importantly: the body can break, and the injuries can be lifelong.

These things had to be learned with time, bitter experience, and suffering.

In my younger, dumber days, I used to let people "have the first shot." Such was my undue confidence. I was also convinced that everyone who started fights or willingly got into fights didn't actually know how to fight. That turned out not to be true. There are people out there who are professional fighters who enjoy starting shit when drunk and high specifically for the thrill of using their skills in what is essentially "justified assault."

So when I met the aforementioned stout Greek student—who, it turned out, had served in the Greek army and could actually fight—I received what we might call in therapy "feedback" from reality.

My assumptions about the world—that I was indestructible, that justice was somehow on my side because I hadn't started the fight—did not pass the "reality test."

My cracked jaw was the feedback needed to knock a hole in

my worldview. It did me some good, but the towering wall of arrogance I lived behind would require a few more knocks yet.

My friends, I now see looking back, started fights knowing that I would assist them. They also did it to enjoy the spectacle of "watching me go." They were not rough types—far from it. They were the wealthy kids of doctors, lawyers, and accountants who lived in mansions in Cheshire with tennis courts and swimming pools. They really just liked the buzz of a tear up—without having to contend with the consequences. When I say "being the one to come off worse" is a recurrent theme in my life, I mean that I was usually some variation of the peacekeeper, burden bearer, or black sheep. If someone were going to get left carrying the can, it would most likely be me.

Why was I willing to sacrifice myself—and my face—for my friends? It's a question I didn't even begin to ask myself until I was in my thirties. By then, I was desperately trying to pull myself out of a spiral of alcohol, drugs, promiscuity, violence, and abusive relationships. The answer, I found, was rooted in my childhood and in a series of poor decisions that sent me careening toward self-destruction when what I really wanted all along was love and safety.

It is the same issue that many of us face today: not being able to love or take care of ourselves properly, not being able to put our needs first, not being able to ask for or go for what we truly want, feeling compelled to attach ourselves to selfish people, and trying to win love from those who cannot offer it.

This doesn't only apply to our personal relationships; it can expand to include our health, our business lives, and even our relationships with our governments. It all comes down to a fractured self, the need to be servile, and the codependent and toxic attachments we form to tyrannical people, institutions, and governing bodies.

I experienced these same problems myself: self-destructive behaviour; trying to please the needs of the worst kinds of people at my own expense; abusive relationships; addictions to sex, violence, and drugs; social anxiety; awkwardness, self-loathing, and depression. In order to solve these problems, I first needed a term to describe their root cause.

I chose the term "codependent." In using this term, I'm going a little beyond the boundaries of the way it is typically used. When I use the term "codependent," I mean a person who is traumatised and brainwashed into needing to be a slave to abusive, psychopathic, narcissistic, tyrannical types of people and systems in order to feel in any way meaningful, visible, or alive.

I mean a person who has been so thoroughly and consistently abused and objectified that they end up colluding in their own self-eradication. That person may have internalised the abuse to such a degree that they will maintain or even further their self-destruction in the absence of the abuser.

Expanding this definition allowed me to understand how I had transformed from a bright, well-educated boy who had been planning to apply to Cambridge into a fat, broken, bitter, nearly homeless bouncer who snorted cocaine off of a house key in a club toilet before returning to work.

So how did I get there so quickly? And then, less quickly, how did I dig myself back out?

First, let's take a deeper look at the classical meaning of the term *codependent*.

Originating from Alcoholics Anonymous meetings, the term referred largely to the partner of an alcoholic who was the "enabler" of the alcoholism. It was a nonclinical definition that some counsellors and therapists used while many others rejected because it could be as confusing as it was enlightening.

Later, in the '80s, the term gained popularity in bestselling pop psychology books in the USA to describe women who were "over giving" in relationships and "lacked boundaries."

Janet G. Woititz's *Adult Children of Alcoholics* came out in 1983, sold two million copies, and stayed on the *New York Times* best-seller list for forty-eight weeks. Robin Norwood's *Women Who Love Too Much* (1985) sold two and a half million copies and spawned twelve-step groups across the country for women addicted to men. Melody Beattie popularized the concept of codependency in 1986 with the book *Codependent No More,* which sold eight million copies. These wildly successful books in the '80s massively increased the usage of the term *codependency,* though they are now sometimes viewed a bit sniffily by the academic community as being "popularised by self-help gurus." The consensus at the time was that the term became overused, misapplied, and eventually misused. Nowadays, it's understood to be a layman's term for *hyperagreeableness* and possibly a clinically diagnosable dependent personality disorder. Today in psychology, the term *codependent* might raise a few eyebrows but is not wildly controversial, and everyone knows what you mean if you use it.

What do I mean when I say it, and why do I use it?

When I think of a codependent state, I visualise two circles overlapping.

Each circle represents a person, and as the circles overlap, each person has entered the other's space. When we have two people in each other's spaces, we have weaknesses in key areas: boundaries, sense of self, agency, sovereignty, responsibility, assertiveness, directness, clarity, emotional regulation, and independence.

When I think about sovereignty or independence, I think of an unbroken circle that stands alone: here we have an unbroken perimeter and no porous or weak boundaries. Like a single cell that is functional, the good things that the cell needs to nourish itself stay inside, and the bad things that are toxic to the cell stay outside where they belong.

When I visualise the two circles overlapping, sometimes I imagine a strong circle drawn with a thick line overlapping with a weak circle whose perimeter is drawn with dots. I think of the strong, dominant circle dwarfing and overpowering the smaller, weaker circle. This represents a codepenent relationship becoming truly toxic and even abusive.

The unbroken circle is independent. The overlapping circles—one being submissive and the other parasitic—are codependent.

In my opinion, there is no such thing as a neutral state of codependency. When boundaries are infringed upon and we are in each other's spaces or carrying each other's loads, I believe that the situation is always somewhere on the spectrum of toxicity and manipulation.

Imagine a scenario wherein a girl aged twenty-six decides it's time to settle down and get with an older, more responsible man to build a future together. She finds a guy aged thirty-five who has a job, is charming and charismatic, and says he wants a family one day. When they actually move in together, however, she finds that on a daily basis his actions reflect a desire not for long-term future building but for passing pleasure: drinking with friends, playing video games, and going out to restaurants. He doesn't seem to save money and isn't interested in her conversations about mortgages or pension schemes.

In an effort to make the relationship work, she then begins to pick up his slack. After all, he is not abusive. Maybe he just needs a nudge in the right direction? At that moment, to "help him be an adult," she has chosen to carry his responsibilities for him. Whatever happens next in this story—be it three months later or thirteen years later with kids involved—she will feel the weight of resentment for doing his adulting for him. He, of course, will remain blissfully unaware. Instead of reciprocating or meeting her where she is, he will simply let this happen, thinking, *Wow, my girl is so cool. She does this so that I can just chill.*

It's not dramatic or film-worthy; technically, it's not even abuse...but it's absolutely a codependent relationship and will lead to terrible problems in the future.

Going back to our two circles, we can see that the small circle represents the codependent victim. But the two circles are *both* engaged in a codependent mode of being. Does that mean that the big circle—the abuser or predator—is codependent? In my view, any person who is not openly expressing their intent in an adult way and whose sense of self or purpose in the world is dependent on a singular other or multiple others is indeed codependent. Not all would agree.

The small circle in our overlapping circles is what I call an "Echo." It does not self-direct and is not attached to its own source. It is like a moon reflecting the light of the Sun. It does not radiate for itself; it only reflects. The big circle radiates light, but its light cannot be seen without a reflection. That's where the small circle comes in.

I contend that, through extensive abuse and trauma, a person is effectively "gutted"—only to then be "stuffed" with someone else's intent, purpose, and identity. We can imagine our small circle, the Codependent Echo, being completely infiltrated and erased by our big circle. Whatever should be inside the small circle has been eradicated by a persistent and consistent bombing campaign of the scorched-earth variety.

This leaves the Codependent Echo existing without truly living. They effectively haunt the shell of their lives and personalities. They can be whatever their environment needs them to be because they have been gutted of their true selves.

In adapting to the traumatic onslaught, they both self-eradicate and learn to be so extremely personally flexible that there is barely any self left at all. In effect, the true Codependent Echo must be whatever the environment needs them to be, and any shred left of "true self" would only impair that performance.

This idea is now quite a distance away, I'm sure you can see, from the idea of someone merely "overhelping" or enabling a drug, alcohol, or gambling addict. This is a way of not-being in the world. No authentic self, no true identity, the eternal ghostly chameleon. Ready to show up as whomever, however, whenever to fix everyone else's problems and to make everything okay. For others. Never for themselves.

So what happens to a person who has experienced abuse in this way? Often, he or she will fall back into one or more of four primitive responses: Fight, Fawn, Flight, or Freeze. These four trauma responses were defined by Pete Walker in his book *Complex PTSD: From Surviving to Thriving*, and they can help us to better understand codependent behaviour.

A Fighter approaches triggering situations combatively and aggressively as an enemy to be overwhelmed.

A Fawner seeks to negotiate and trade his or her way out of a position of danger, making endless compromises to keep the peace.

In a Flight response, we simply run away. This could be disappearing into our work or hobbies, avoiding conflict and responsibility, or physically leaving situations that become taxing.

A Freezer is stuck in place, hoping the predator won't see him or her. This manifests as dissociating or becoming numb. This might lead to overeating, using drugs, watching too much TV, gambling, or anything that allows a person to get out of his or her own mind.

Three of these trauma responses—Fight, Freeze, and Flight—have long been recognised by the scientific community. The Fawn response, which is the predominant trauma response experienced by people who are codependent, was first identified by Pete Walker. He struggles with complex PTSD as well as codependency, and these experiences have given him an authentic, deep understanding of this subject.

Given this information, I'd like to build upon my definition of what it means to be Echo Codependent:

- Having a desperate, unconscious need to submit to and serve a tyrannical partner or institution
- Having a pronounced primary Fawn response

It is possible to have a secondary trauma response. For example, one might experience Fawn and Flight or Fawn and Freeze, but the predominant trauma response must be to Fawn in order to qualify as Echo Codependent under this definition.

While trauma responses such as these may be psychologically hardwired into us, experiencing a Fawn response over a lifetime will inevitably lead to strong feelings of resentment, anger, self-loathing, impotence, immaturity, and frustration.

In the following chapters, we will explore how to overcome bad relationships and avoid them in the future. I will give you the tools to defeat Echo Codependency once and for all, and I will outline the ways in which your sense of self can improve by recognising and eliminating toxicity.

Overcoming Echo Codependency is the first step toward becoming a functional adult. I will include philosophical wisdom that will allow you to grow and thrive as a human being in peace and authenticity. My own understanding of codependency has been shaped and expanded by such diverse studies as Buddhism, Taoism, martial arts, and the writings of Nietzsche. In these next chapters, I will share my insights with you.

Being rigorously honest with ourselves and with others is the only way to be. If we put aside all our needs and wants and only show up to fulfil the needs of others, we are not living honest and authentic lives. Codependence is a sickness, and not one of us consented to it.

CHAPTER 2

HOW TO "TRAUMA BOND" A CHILD

THE TOUGH THING ABOUT BEING A CHILD IN AN ABUSIVE scenario is the lack of credit cards and a car. If things get a little dramatic at home, you don't have the option to say, "Well, Mary-Beth, I can see you are in one of your tempers. I'll go stay at the Holiday Inn for two nights while you settle your nerves."

As a child, this just isn't one of our options.

Because we are young and unlearned in the rules of this domain called the "adult world," we lack the ability to distinguish the precise meridian between that which is ours and that which belongs to the other.

This means that if Daddy is hitting Mummy—and Daddy is very angry and Mummy is very upset—and I am very scared, as a small child, little of these differentiations are drawn. At this point in the child's development, there is no fully formed ego with strong boundaries. There is no strong, distinct sense of "I" versus "other."

Or, in head shrinker lingo, there is no boundary between the subject (the child observing or experiencing violence) versus the object (the primary caregiver doing the violence). Therefore to a child: I am he who hits, I am she who is hit, I am the house in which the hitting takes place. It is all one. I am, in traumatised infant logic, the whole stinking chaotic mess, and therefore, I am responsible for it. If it is all me, then it must be mine, and I must have some agency over what happened or is happening.

The bewildering feelings of guilt and shame that victims of childhood abuse feel from being raised in chaotic, abusive environments can be explained by this logic of malignant unity. One can be abused by an adult and simultaneously feel guilt and shame for the abuse inflicted, even though one had no say in it and no capacity to stop it, fight back, or escape.

A traumatic, unsafe household is a hellish penitentiary for a child. A dark, torturous space full of suffering, foreboding, and the shying away from shadows, lest they be a device of suffering or humiliation. If you were raised in adverse conditions, this will account for why you shy away from people, places, and scenarios. Why you can appear to be introverted or isolation-seeking, and why you struggle to ask for what you want.

I personally wasn't a big fan of being a child. It wasn't the best of times for me. No credit cards, no car, no size-weight-training advantage to hit the abusers in the head with a jumping elbow. Indeed, like all children, I was impotent to protect myself and impotent to protect others from being abused. Sometimes I was literally forced to watch.

Films that force one to watch people suffer abuse are hard for everyone, except for the truly psychopathic, but those who have lived that fantasy as a reality may find it somewhat more stressful. I know I certainly do. I mean films that involve torture, genocide, enslavement, kidnapping, sexual abuse, gulags, or concentration camps. For some, these are an opportunity to safely experience the darker elements of a distant life belonging to someone else. I find it pretty hard going. People tell me I'm unusually sensitive. Maybe.

Sometimes I wonder, though: maybe everyone else is unusually insensitive? It can't always be me who's at fault.

Anyway, back to the child's growth process in a toxic environment. Spikes of adrenaline from surges of terror, shame, and humiliation definitely have a long-term impact on the person and their ego boundaries. Extreme abuse, like strong psychedelics or near-death experiences, are boundary-dissolving.

The trauma knocks holes in your boundary walls. Boundaries are good. Like a single-celled organism, the rule is simple: good stuff stays in; crap stays out. When the boundaries are broken, we end up with good stuff seeping out and crap stuff seeping in.

What does this mean for a person? What could this mean for you if you have survived such circumstances?

You would, at the very least, struggle to maintain divisions mentally, emotionally, and practically between your thoughts and your feelings and between your needs and the needs of others. You would experience a continual boundary-dissolving effect.

I've had a skin bacterial infection a couple of times from doing Brazilian Jiu Jitsu on dirty mats. As you scrabble about, you naturally scuff your knees and elbows. If enough sweat and dirt have seeped into the mat, the crapola will get into those scuffs and scrapes. You don't even need to be bleeding; it's enough if the top layer of skin has been shorn off. It's called impetigo. The problem with the sores is that they struggle to heal normally, causing them to remain open as though sending a signal to the skin to not heal as usual. A sort of ongoing dissolution of the skin boundary.

If you had your boundaries dissolved through traumatic abuse, you can think of the broken and unbroken circles, the single-celled entities we mentioned in the first chapter. It follows naturally that chaotic childhood conditions would lead to the broken circle attaching to another circle, creating codependency.

The boundary between what you are feeling and what others are feeling may become dissolved. What would this mean?

It would mean that, in adulthood, you would be confused if someone else were feeling an emotion that you were not also feeling. If someone else were angry, for example, you might assume it was in some way your responsibility. If you automatically tend to think this, then you have a dissolved boundary around the distinction between your emotions and others'.

I know this because I lived this in childhood and in adulthood.

Tyrannical, domineering parents who demand that you carry their feelings for them carve out your young heart and force their bitter, messed-up adult feelings into a space not yet designed for it. This may result in you being "very mature for your age" or becoming "parentified"—being forced through parental negligence or coercion into being the parent in your household—possibly for your siblings (to alleviate the lazy parent's responsibility) or even for the parent(s) themselves (to mother your own mother as it were).

This strays rapidly into the realm of emotional incest. Where actual incest is a sexual infraction between family members, emotional incest is where the target is covertly coerced into offering the type of emotional support (or to be a whipping post) that should only ever be offered by a similarly aged adult. Both encroach on boundaries—one physical and sexual, the other psychological and emotional.

What impact do these things have on a human? Well, it warps our formation. We don't develop as we should. We end up accommodating and "learning to live with" the abuse. We become accommodating, responsibility-taking, shut-up-and-put-up-with-it types.

This creates in us survival mechanisms. These appear to us, subjectively, as spontaneous and naturally occurring modes of being able to cope with the environment we are in. Because we are children, we have no way of being able to draw the boundary and make the judgment that "this is abuse!" We simply haven't watched the TV shows, read the books, or listened to the podcasts to know what abuse consists of. For us, it's just normal family life.

But it's crucial to make the distinction. To say, "I didn't do that—it wasn't my choice," and, "That was absolutely an act of appalling abuse."

If we can't make these two simple statements, we will be forever trapped in the domain of thinking everything is our fault and that nothing anyone who loves us does can ever be deliberately abusive. It renders it all "an error" or a "result of their own childhood trauma."

As a child, I learned to love science fiction, fantasy, and books on personal development and psychology from a very early age. From the age of twelve, I began to fall in love with an interest that combined all of these: martial arts.

At first, martial arts were a terrible burden to me. I was forced to go to karate when my family moved to Portugal when I was eight. I trained in Quarteira with a ferocious Portuguese gentleman called Jose Verissimo in Shito Ryu. At that age, I did not like violence, aggression, or competition and found it generally stressful.

Later, I was pushed into doing Japanese Jiu Jitsu, and occasionally the jiu jitsu and karate schools would do seminars with a group of ninjutsu students who would come over from Spain. Yes, I know this sounds absurd, but I have trained on the beach in Quarteira with men in bright white gis from karate and jiu jitsu schools working together with Spanish ninjas dressed in black. In broad daylight. We threw shuriken into some boards. It was actually quite fun despite getting sand in my gi.

None of it really clicked for me though. My parents and my

family, in general, are sports fanatics and compete at a pretty decent level in many arenas. But I had had the competition whipped out of me at some point. I suspect the demands placed on me by the adults around me—people who were impatient, selfish, alcoholic, hypercompetitive, narcissistic bullies with anger management issues—may have had something to do with that.

That was until I was sent to boarding school. My school, Queens College in Taunton, was a good school, I'd say. It was odd, but English boarding school culture is odd. The thing that changed martial arts from something other people made me do into something I wanted to do was the casual violence at the school.

At thirteen, I had been used to a very liberal, freewheeling life, where I was allowed to do what I wanted, and not only was I permitted to speak to people from multiple backgrounds, classes, and ages, I was expected to as my father was in sales and we were often invited to meetings and events. I was trained to talk to everyone. I had also been exposed to women—or perhaps I should say they had been exposed to me. It was a beachy, sunshine life in Portugal, and in the '80s, from what I recall, it was pretty sexually liberal.

So when I arrived at a dour, po-faced, religious boarding school, it was something of a culture shock. For me *and* for them. I was beyond precocious. We did not get on at first at all, and I got into a lot of trouble. However, after a term or so, I figured it out and actually came to enjoy being there.

The problem was that casual violence was pretty rampant. By all accounts, the prefects in the years above us had been through vicious hazing that, following a bit of a scandal, the school had clamped down on, but the boys themselves were still fond of smacking each other—and especially the younger kids—around.

We had an environment where there were predators and there were prey. The few years of semicontact sparring I had done in karate and jiu jitsu was better than the absolute zero training of the boys around me, so even with the older guys, word got around that I would fight if attacked.

As you read this, it may sound petty. But remember something: institutions like boarding schools are petty in their essence because the institution is a mini world, consisting of fiefdoms and squabbles over territory, in which pecking orders naturally form. People get peculiarly invested in small bits of psychological space. That's why having a reputation at age thirteen for being "tough" meant a lot. Here I began to attribute status to martial arts training. Previously it had been nothing but a dreadful bore; now it made me cool and interesting. This shift in attitude to my martial arts training happened to coincide with a pretty nasty fight response that I was developing that helped to protect me from predators. Reputations are easily built in small institutions. I think it's called being a "big fish in a small pond." Soon, I was that kid from a foreign country who would "flip out" if messed with and "knew kung fu or something." Trauma, status, and agency came together to give me focus on a subject I had previously resisted.

Let's look more closely at this Fight response I had developed. According to Pete Walker in his excellent book *Complex PTSD: From Surviving to Thriving*, when we are faced with extremely traumatic situations that we cannot escape, we begin to develop primitive defence mechanisms. These are primitive in two senses: in the sense of being unfitted to the needs of modern life, so ultimately, self-destructive (this is called "maladaptive" in psych lingo) and also in the sense of coming from an earlier time in our evolutionary history.

These responses have been incorporated into a useful model of the 4Fs:

Fight—an anger/aggression response whereby we meet the threat and attack it (this threat may be real or perceived). Shows up as being confrontational, bullying, and explosive emotionally.

Flight—the threat or stress-perceived-as-existential-threat appears, and our primitive tendency is to run away and escape. Shows up as a tendency to bail at the first sign of trouble. Any coping strategy that is escape-dependent, e.g., gambling, porn, drinking, drugs, work, fantasising compulsively, and/or zoning out (called dissociation). Any form of detachment from reality, rather than a psychotic loss of reality, puts a person on the sliding scale of dissociation. This psychological phenomenon could merely be mild emotional detachment from the immediate circumstances or range through to an inability to function effectively in the world due to a severe disconnection from physical and psychological experience.

Freeze—the threat appears, and we keep still. As some predators have eyesight that is movement-dependent, keeping still and blending into the background can sometimes work. This can show up as feelings of laziness, procrastination, depression, or a straightforward desire to keep still. I suspect some over-eaters want to be so full that they can't move, and this could be a Freeze response to threat-stress.

And then there is the special one. This must have taken place later in our evolution and is not a lizard brain response. It requires mammalian prefrontal cortex development. It is also the main focus of my concept of codependency, and how I engage in an effort to bring people "back to themselves" so that they can regain agency in their own lives.

It is the Fawn response.

Fawn—we try to trade with the aggressor. This for that. We seek compromise, become peacekeepers, and try to allay the threat based on "pleasing" the threat with a trade-off. This is the beginning of people-pleaser syndrome, which, when it is learned from childhood and seeps into one's DNA, metaphorically speaking, is the core component of codependency, as I'm describing it.

In my life, as a child coming through various kinds of physical, sexual, and psychological abuse and desperately trying to find out how to be in the world, rage was already something I had learned to switch on and off to keep aggressors at bay. Fawning was something that I had implicitly been trained to do when trying to trade with parental figures whose rules and moods were as mercurially unpredictable as their interest in parenting me. I was also explicitly trained to be "pleasing." To be "a little adult" and to charm people.

Sadly for me, the people who have a primary response of Fight and a secondary response of Fawn tend to be highly narcissistic. Indeed the aggression and ingratiation polarity is the yin-yang of the narcissistic personality disordered person's mode of being in the world.

But wait a minute, you may well ask, does that mean I'm reading a book by a narcissist? No, but I have an intimate understanding of the NPD (narcissistic personality disorder) mode of being, and I suspect that's why I have had so many malignant narcissists in my life.

But hang on, didn't you say you were a lifelong codependent? And that you have CPTSD (complex posttraumatic stress disorder)? Aren't these the opposite of narcissism? Aren't codependents with CPTSD always the victims of narcissists?

I get these kinds of questions all the time over on my YouTube channel, and they need a little further explanation.

First of all, this isn't "rock, paper, scissors," and I'm afraid, despite what you might read or learn online or what you have imbibed from our current cultural obsession with victimhood, being the victim of a "wholly evil devil" does not render you or anyone else a "wholly pure angel." Far from it.

To break this down step by step: narcissism is absolutely an expression of CPTSD.

CPTSD was defined by Judith Herman in 1992 as a condition distinct from PTSD (posttraumatic stress disorder) because it depends on a different type of trauma. Type 1 (PTSD) would be a big singular event. Type 2 (CPTSD) would be a series of smaller events that take place over time and cannot be escaped.

I would add to this definition that a PTSD event can typically be recalled visually, auditorily, and kinaesthetically, i.e., the client can remember the event, what they heard, what they saw, what they felt, etc.

A CPTSD event is typically much harder to be recalled with visual or auditory memories, so only the emotions are recalled. This is confusing to the client as an emotion absent a connected memory will be experienced subjectively as a spontaneously occurring emotion pertaining to something in the present.

Now, I know people will say, "I have PTSD, and I don't recall everything." My personal opinion is that there is not now—nor has there ever been—anyone who has PTSD without CPTSD or vice versa. Trauma is trauma. If you don't recall everything, I would explore the possibility of CPTSD. The label doesn't matter that much as the road to recovery for people with PTSD and CPTSD is so similar.

According to Pete Walker, author of *Complex PTSD: From Surviving to Thriving*, if the Fight type of trauma response goes unchecked, the child will grow up believing that the best way to secure love and safety in the world is by aggressively bullying it out of his or her targets. The narcissistic personality is a primary Fight, secondary Fawn responder. They can switch between bullying and charming their targets into giving them the adulation they crave. Sam Vaknin, author of *Malignant Self Love: Narcissism Revisited*, has also drawn a correlation between complex posttraumatic stress and the formation of NPD as a defence to traumatic environments. He even goes on to suggest that NPD can only be treated effectively when viewed as a CPTSD response.

This is a problematic position for some people who struggle to break out of the "narcissist as pure evil abuser" mindset. But the truth is that, through tracing the formation of NPD in childhood, we can see what types of abuse the child endured by the defence mechanisms they create, like grandiosity and lack of empathy.

Now to the codependency issue: surely I cannot be claiming that a narcissist is a codependent?

I absolutely am.

The essence of codependency is needing other people in order to have a sense of self. There is such a thing as predatory codependency, in which the narcissist codependent bullies, entraps, and cajoles the target or targets into giving them what they need: attention.

There is also prey codependency, in which the hyperagreeable Fawn responder sacrifices or martyrs themself at the altar of the other's needs to get what they themself need: a sense of significance through martyrdom.

Both are jealous, resentful, and flooded with feelings of guilt and shame. The predatory codependent suppresses the guilt and shame, which are then sublimated (changed unconsciously) into feelings of aggression, fantasies of dominance and grandeur, plans for vengeance, and a need to dominate the other. The other is insignificant and utterly replaceable.

The prey codependent suppresses their jealousy and resentment and is guided by strong feelings of guilt. They fight like

hell to feel every single droplet of guilt. The jealousy is sublimated into sadomasochism, trying to do so much that others
notice their selflessness, a desire to control and manipulate
other people's feelings and reactions, and a need to be utterly
submissive without restraint to the other. The other they select
has the most significance and, to the prey codependent, could
never be replaced.

If you picked up this book hoping to have your ego stroked about
what a good, virtuous empath you are, the bad news is that you
are most likely stuck in a cycle of agency denial in order to
stay invisible and to avoid the responsibility of being an adult
human being. It's not your fault, but there is only one person in
this world who can fix it. Nobody is coming to save you.

When I dove into martial arts, I did it from a desire to fight
back, to protect myself from predators, and to have some kind
of significance. I didn't realise that fragile narcissism was written into the source code of martial arts themselves. What do I
mean by "fragile narcissism"? The classic narcissist is overtly
grandiose. The fragile or vulnerable narcissist is covering for
a defensive, reactionary grandiosity that is predominantly a
shield for deep feelings of inadequacy. It was a peer of Freud
and Jung, Alfred Adler, who coined the term "inferiority complex." This meant that due to some childhood sense of one's
own impotence, weakness, or defect, we would feel an urge to
compensate for that in some way.

This isn't to say martial arts are worthless. In fact, when my
benevolent dictatorship begins a few years after the inevitable
collapse of our civilisation, I will insist on everyone learning
martial arts so that they are less repressed, more confident, less

cowardly, and more rooted in their own bodies. But we must watch for fragile narcissism. It's harder to detect and worse in some ways than classic narcissism.

People always ask what martial arts I did. It's a natural question; I'd ask the same thing. I mention karate and Japanese Jiu Jitsu. As I studied through the '90s and fell in love with Bruce Lee, I wanted to explore Jeet Kune Do (Bruce Lee's style) and all of his recommendations: this included kickboxing, Muay Thai, wrestling, silat, tai chi, and wing chun. By the time I went to university in 1996, MMA was gaining popularity, but back then we would call it Vale Tudo, cage fighting, or shootfighting. Fortunately, in Birmingham there was ample opportunity to study these different styles. Back then, as a generalisation, Liverpool was more strictly a boxing and kickboxing city with some notable karate legends. Birmingham was a larger, more cosmopolitan city and more niche styles were accessible.

Why do I say fragile narcissism is written into the source code of martial arts and that we should train but be wary of it? The best way to look at this, I think, is to reduce martial arts to its components as rationally as possible in order to look at what it claims to be and what it actually is.

Martial arts relates to the god Mars and, as such, relates to war arts. I don't know about you, but I learned nothing in my martial arts training that pertained to modern warfare directly. So straight off the bat, it's not got inside of it what it claims to have on the tin. Very few things actually do in this life, it seems to me.

What actually is martial arts in practise? Typically, it is some kind of syllabus that prioritises, to varying degrees, history, culture, practical self-defence, and personal development. These things do not often complement each other. In fact, they more often than not directly get in each other's way.

An example off the top of my head: I studied aikido when I was fifteen. It is often advertised as being an effective form of self-defence. I went to a dojo in Birkenhead, where they wore a silly white ultra-heavy keikogi and a black hakama (the traditional split skirt). There I learned how to deal with being grabbed on the wrist. All of my defences were circular because the creator of the style wanted a physical manifestation of a spiritual concept related to infinity, nature, God, and spirit. Blend the energy, move in a way where your chi or ki flows, do as little harm to the opponent as possible, circle your arms, spin your body, and flow.

Okay. Now put me in a pub down the road from the dojo, and let's see how it plays out.

A local miscreant eyeballs me and decides I'm easy picking. He gets in my face and yells. I can smell his breath. He is swearing, high, drunk, clearly psychotic, and I am scared. Does he grab my wrist from four feet away whilst doing a lunge with most of his weight over the lunging leg? Does he do a chop from up to down mirroring the move of a Japanese katana to strike me a blow on the top of my skull?

No, he headbutts me and hits me with a glass on the side of my face.

Where is my aikido?

Now, I loved aikido, so I studied it. I read a book written by the founder's grandson and translated into English, in which he revealed that aikido is not to be taught as self-defence but a system of spiritual growth rooted in tough, vigorous training through which the martial art (contact side) would manifest the founder's obsession with traditional Japanese weaponry (bokken and bo) and circular movement. Of equal importance are cold water baths, restricted dieting and fasting, no alcohol or drugs, and a very physical, rigorous form of Shinto-Buddhism to bring about spiritual growth.

The founder was not creating a pub brawling style. This is specifically mentioned in his grandson's book. The founder, Morihei Ueshiba, knew what brawling was. He called the snapping of bones, gouging of eyes, and headbutting common to street fighting or the battlefield "Bugei." He felt that, though this material worked, it was degenerative to the spirit of the practitioner whom he wanted to elevate spiritually. He wanted his practitioners to elevate, transcend, and grow with "Budo."

So why are we putting a square peg in a round hole? And why are people learning aikido but not fasting, cold water dunking, or explicitly training very, very rigorously only for the spiritual benefits?

I would claim that, in this world we live in, the reasons are ideological. It could be claimed that this happens because people are hucksters looking to make a buck, but this has never made sense to me. Making money through martial arts is very tough. I know because I did it for a decade. It's more like a kind of religious thinking that takes place. We have "faith" in our martial arts, which means we wilfully suspend our disbelief and critical thinking in order to receive some sort of promised utopian benefits off in the wonderful future.

This, I'm afraid, is a delusion. This is one half of why I say fragile narcissism is written into the source code of martial arts and why so many (certainly not all) instructors and people involved in martial arts are so highly narcissistic.

Narcissism depends on delusion. I know it's typically thought of as more about selfishness and abusive behaviour, but those are only symptoms. They are manifestations of the structure—not the structure itself. If you focus only on the things that hurt you, your understanding will remain superficial, and you will be frustrated and vulnerable to getting back into another narcissistic relationship.

The narcissist is in a world of delusion. So is the martial artist. They are essentially LARPing (live action role play—you know, the people who do historical reenactments or dress up as orcs and elves and hit each other with plastic axes) and pretending to have a superpower.

"It's not a superpower! That's silly!" I hear you cry. Well, okay. Just listen to the claims of martial arts instructors themselves. What are they training you to do? If you give them money, time, and dedication, what do you get in return? The hope that someone grabs you by the wrist in a street fight so that you can flow with their motion and put them in an armlock that they won't resist?

It's a delusion of grandeur. The fact is, fighting is really dangerous. You can train very hard for a very long time, and you will find that, scientifically speaking, you hit a point of diminishing returns very early on.

Can you do with your hands the damage a Glock can do? No.

How do you think you would fare if you were rushed by ten grown men who were angry, committed to hurting you, and high on drugs and you were armed with a Glock? You've got fifteen rounds. Do you fantasise that you would shoot them all dead before they made contact with you? You've never been on a range. Watch some footage of shootings. Watch how quickly people can cover distance. Watch how quickly even a trained person can be overwhelmed and disarmed. Watch how many nine-millimetre rounds a grown male can take before stopping. It's sobering, truly.

It's delusional. It's grandiose. And it's narcissistic in its essence.

The explosion of interest in MMA has sobered the martial arts community somewhat, and to some degree, people are less likely to be so fantastical in their estimations now. But they are still off the charts. Why?

The frail human ego. We **all** have to live inside a little bit of blue pill delusion to get through the day. Someone who was perpetually in contact with the realities of potential risk would become very nonresilient and anxious in their worldview very quickly. It's the extent to which we let this delusional, blue pill overconfidence take over that's the issue.

I love martial arts, but I would never steep myself in them ever again and will stick to the sportive elements. Muay Thai is good fun, and I prefer smashing the bags to running. There is, for many people, a repetition compulsion in martial arts. A repetition compulsion is a Freudian concept that means we act out distressing circumstances again and again unconsciously. Many believe that there is also a blind hope for a different outcome. I believe many traumatised, bullied people are using martial arts to try to seek vengeance in the present on long dead ghosts from their pasts. This is where the faith, culture, history, and ideological elements creep in. It's as if we believe some faraway—in time and geography—magical-spell-based superpower system, with its own costumes, rituals, and foreign words, will save us from the trauma of our pasts.

To this extent, it can be a very unhealthy endeavour and might prolong our inability to process our pain by giving us a means to cope with our cowardice: we pretend we are facing our demons in the dojo, but it's merely a performative gesture replacing the actual encounter with our own grief.

The past is gone. Beating up a bully in a bar today because you were abused many years ago has no therapeutic benefit whatsoever. I know. I've run the experiment many, many times.

Train hard, enjoy your training, and be realistically prepared for real-world violence if you feel you live in a context where it behoves you to do so, but never, ever fail to meet reality just as it is with courage.

CHAPTER 3

FROM ESCAPE TO ENLIGHTENMENT

I WAS BORN IN ONE OF THE MOST NORMAL PLACES IN THE United Kingdom. My hometown is the perfectly unremarkable Bebington. This is a village on the Wirral, a postindustrial, semirural peninsula near Liverpool.

I do not have many fond memories of home life from my childhood. I did not feel wanted. I felt, instead, like a burden. If there was a problem, it was my fault. Nothing was ever good enough, and I could never do anything that would win me love or safety. I had everything a kid could want materially, but I never felt truly loved.

One of my earliest childhood memories was of struggling with feelings of overwhelming guilt. There were a few times I put myself to bed with no dinner as a punishment. When my mother would look for me, she would find me in bed with a cup of water next to me. I believe this self-inflicted excommunication from the household came from a deeply felt perception that I had brought tremendous stress to my parents' relationships and that I was unwelcome and unwanted in my home. A pest and a burden.

The stress of the environment gave me alopecia nervosa. After a particularly severe bout of terror-inducing screaming and shaming, clumps of my hair started to fall out.

Alopecia nervosa is a condition in which sustained stress leads to hair falling out in clumps. After being screamed at by one or the other raging parent seeking to dump their stress after some minor infraction (dropping a cup, playing too loudly, making a face they didn't like), I would fall into a state of frozen terror in which my limbs would go tingly and numb. I would struggle to breathe, and the bedroom I had been sent to would seem to expand to enormous proportions. The floor would tilt, and the distance from my duvet cover to the window would seem endless. Dissociation or freezing is often the first response of the psychologically abused child as none of the other responses are available to them.

I remember feeling enormous guilt for existing and frequently wishing that my existence, and the stress it obviously caused, would cease.

Did my parents love each other? There was little evidence of this. If they had loved each other, it was before I was born.

They seemed locked into a pretty nasty power battle from as young as I can remember.

Their relationship dynamic could be most easily characterised as that between Gandalf and the Balrog. In order to help the Hobbits escape, Gandalf, the wizard hero of the story *The Lord of the Rings*, sacrifices himself by entering into a fight with a huge, fiery, demonic entity called a Balrog.

In the story, the two fall off a bridge in battle and tumble into the depths, locked together in mutual hate, brawling and snapping at one another all the way down. In this metaphor, my parents were both Balrogs. Huge, fiery, terrifying, and indestructible.

The tense environment was unbearable to me, and I felt extremely guilty because I believed that I had caused it. My birth was the burden. I knew it. My parents argued a lot, and I knew the topics were money and responsibility. My father, seeking to escape what he perceived to be the prison of a false life in which he was married to a woman he didn't want to marry and had children he did not want, was a serial philanderer. He confirmed this to me whilst drunk twenty years later. He'd married my mother because it was "easier to get by in life if you had a wife" and had me and my sister "because that's what she demanded of me." My father did not want me. He already had had two sons in his first marriage. And my mother, a wayward and headstrong twenty-something, clearly felt I was ruining the party.

This feeling of extreme psychological pressure meant that I often looked for a means of escape. I found it in books, films, and fantasies into which I would plunge as deeply as I could and hide there. Deep in Narnia, beyond the wardrobe, I would stay as long as I could. Because my reading was voracious and driven by fear, I ended up with an adult reading level. My refuge was in strange worlds, far, far away: often bizarre and terrifying places in and of themselves but where the characters were at least coherent and occasionally even acted in good faith with a degree of honour.

In these fantasy narratives, even the bad characters could be understood. The worlds they inhabited were predictable, and their wrongdoings were predicated on certain rules. In my world, it was the lack of coherence and structure that damaged me the most. There were no rules I could adhere to that would allay punishment, guilt-tripping, shaming, smacking, or screaming fits of rage directed at me.

A worldview formed for me in Bebington in the early '80s. It seemed very ugly and very hostile, and my sense was that the ugliness and hostility were not necessary but almost self-inflicted. Even at a young age I could see there was needless disharmony and a flagrant taste for bitterness and pettiness. What, I wondered to myself, could be the problem?

Adults.

Adults were the problem. Oddly shaped creatures, twisted into uncomfortable pretensions and practises, who were poorly dressed (it was the early '80s, a real sartorial dip), ill-tempered, uncomfortable in their own skins, dangerously quick-tempered, and lacking in anything approximating grace. Adults were pompous, pale, demanding, and sinister. They had strange rules and demands that, even when met, never made them relaxed or happy.

Yes, I was surrounded by some misery-addicted, hostile moth-erfuckers in the northwest of England in 1984. And they loved sharing that misery around. And how they loathed to see others happy. Even children.

In my childhood days, I noticed a strange attitude towards myself and other children. Some adults were happy when children were happy, but the majority seemed to be irritated and inflamed by children's happiness. They also clearly enjoyed bellowing and bullying children to feel more powerful.

I remember in my school when I was about six years old, the headmaster came into our class to play guitar and sing to us. Why he had chosen to do this on this particular day I know not. It wasn't standard operational procedure. Perhaps he had been dumped. Perhaps he wanted a captive audience to per-form to so he could fulfil his Bob Dylan fantasy. When he sang, we children all listened. At one point, I took my friend's action figure (a dinosaur-headed man creature) and made him dance across the desk in time to the music. The headmaster saw this as mockery and had a screaming fit. He stormed out of the room proclaiming that I, personally, had "ruined everything." This only confirmed to me that adults were dangerous, fragile, and prone to temper tantrums—and were best avoided.

The world looked like hell to me. I obsessively drew swirling spirals of dark energy and pictures of naked and chained men and women being flung screaming into these maelstroms. I drew mazes in which humans were perpetually trapped and monsters with claw-toothed mouths eternally consuming screaming souls.

I became aggressive. At some point I started torturing my toys. I had quite a collection of *Star Wars* figures that would face my sadism. Why? Probably because I couldn't do anything else. I couldn't fight back because that would lead to more pain, but I still felt compelled to model the hostility and cruelty of the adults around me.

My driving belief at this time was that the world was diseased and must be escaped at all costs.

As I grew older and my agency increased, my access to books improved. A particular step up in this access was when I was sent to boarding school at age thirteen. At the age of seven, my family had left the UK so that my father could pursue a career as a time-share salesman in Portugal. When my school in Vale do Lobo was condemned to be knocked down in order to expand a more lucrative golf course, my parents decided to send me back to the UK. I went to live with a great-aunt in Taunton, Somerset.

I have to say this was also a strange, humiliating, and boundary-breaking experience for me. My upbringing in Portugal up to that point had been very "liberal." I was allowed to mix with other expat kids of all ages, and my friend group was a multinational group of kids all the way up to eighteen years old.

To then be sent to a dour, strict, religious boarding school hell-bent on conformity was a bit of a shock to my young system to say the least. Uniforms were unknown to me. As were the excess of rules, pettiness, bitterness, and intergenerational violence and sexual abuse that were commonplace there. If an older boy told you to do something, you must do it. If a prefect told you to do it, it was gospel. If a teacher told you, it was as though Gabriel himself had decreed your fate.

This was a world where other teenage boys could issue punishments called "fatigues." Fatigues included cleaning prefect rooms, cleaning common areas, collecting and distributing milk across the house, emptying bins, cleaning toilets, and so on. They could also include writing out pages of the Bible, being made to "stand out" (standing in place facing the wall in a public place in silence), or simply being beaten on the arms and legs. If I didn't do them, up the chain of command it would go.

The world I had been in up until that point had made me precocious and confident. My parents were both involved in sales and the social life that went with it. I was expected to behave as a young adult, to shake people's hands, make eye contact, and speak to them politely and forthrightly. I was expected to impress.

I know what you're thinking: how could I be at once insecure and self-blaming and precocious and confident? Allow me to explain. The formation of narcissistic personality disorder usually takes place between two polarities in which the child is simultaneously told they are bad and useless and that they are wonderful and gifted as long as they perform a function (one that is often inappropriately adult for a child) that benefits the hunger for narcissistic supply the parents feel. In my experience, whilst my childhood had left me feeling worthless and self-blaming, there were moments when my parents heaped praise on me. These moments were when I behaved as a "small adult" either by acting on stage or in social situations where I could seem to project an image of being "wise beyond my years."

Parentification is when parents unconsciously push their children to take on a parental role and fulfil roles that should only be for adults. The child realises they must ignore their own feelings if they wish to feel close to their parents and take over adult tasks. GJ Jurkovic identified "narcissistic parentification" specifically as being the parents' efforts to unconsciously induce the child to conform to their own "ego ideal." *In other words, they force the child to be the adult person they wish they could be.*

All in all, this meant that the blind, Fawning submission required of a boarding school environment was not something I was used to, and I had some rather large run-ins early on in my time there. But I quickly learned the rules and which personalities within the system could easily be manipulated if I coloured within the lines and played the game.

I had a chameleonlike ability to adapt, and my hypervigilant sense of where real danger lay really helped in the creaky halls of Queen's College, Taunton. My traumatic upbringing had made mastering the game in this environment an easy pastime. In the end, I enjoyed my time there.

There were cliques for this and that interest. I managed to get into a group from "School House" (I was "Jack Tigg House") that would, on certain evenings, break into the history classroom to watch videos. There is no way that the history teachers didn't know we were doing it, but we were quiet, careful, and neat. And so the terrible crime of teenage boys watching *Apocalypse Now* or *Aliens* together and then carefully putting everything back in its place was overlooked.

You may know of the Slovenian philosopher Slavoj Žižek who

explains that Stalin permitted and even encouraged jokes to be made at his expense, knowing that these small crimes actually served to enforce his power. Understanding this lesson from an early age helped me immeasurably over the years. I avoided many of the traps and pitfalls I saw others fall into because I knew, at a gut level, which rules absolutely had to be followed and which ones were a little less rigorously enforced. And when these standards changed. For people with Echo Codependency and people-pleaser syndrome, this is a key skill to develop so that we don't end up falling into the twin traps of neurotic naïveté and hyperconscientiousness.

Neurotic naïveté is a term I coined to describe, at first, my own tendency to insist on the most naïve perspectives of the world and ignore all incoming data that would alter that perspective. The outcome of neurotically insisting upon naïveté was that I found myself perpetually saying, "Oh no, I'm so disappointed and feel so let down." Then when I started coaching in 2013, I found this tendency in my clients, so I added it to my list of people-pleaser syndrome traits.

Hyperconscientiousness is a form of perfectionism where, essentially, we take a good trait—like being conscientious or dependable—and try to manifest it in our lives to an absurd degree. There is a limit to how conscientious you can be. It's a form of conscience-based giving, and giving should never be without boundaries or limits.

Apart from enjoying learning to play the game at boarding school, there was unfettered access to books. I could use the library as much as I wanted. And if they didn't have a book I wanted, the librarian was delighted to order it in for me. This was no small consolation for the pain of the liberty I lost there. So when the other boys went home for the weekend, leaving me in a largely empty Hogwarts-meets-army-barracks setup, I would spend hours and hours practising my psychological escape in the school library.

The books I read and reread were Stephen King's *The Dark Tower* and *The Dark Half*, Thomas Harris's *The Silence of the Lambs*, Sir Arthur Conan Doyle's Sherlock Holmes stories, Anthony Burgess's *A Clockwork Orange,* and anything and everything by Clive Barker. These were dark landscapes filled with fascinating creatures (some of these monstrosities were even human) who battled against superior forces for their individuality with the skills they had available to them. In these stories, the darkness these antiheroes and heroes faced was always both internal and external. I can't abide stories of goody-goody heroes fighting pure evil. They make me feel sick, which is why the current spate of Avengers movies leaves me cold. Give me a heroin-addicted narcissist genius like Holmes or a practitioner of social justice combined with cannibalism like Hannibal Lecter any day.

At around that time, one of the other boys who was also often still around on weekends was a chap called Howard. We got on well. He had a weird sense of humour, loved metal and rap as much as I did, and used to lend me his graphic novels to read.

When I was fourteen, he asked me if I would like to try acid. I don't remember how much I took, but it didn't cause me to go berserk. Three of us sat talking, listening to music, tripping gently, and trying to figure out why the leaves on the tree outside the dorm room were moving so strangely in the wind. They were moving outside of their normal pattern. They echoed.

They flashed. It was an overall pleasant experience that piqued my interest in psychedelics, especially the potential doorway they could open to escape this hell-realm, as I saw it then.

It was a gentle experience: tripping my balls off in the Jack Tigg House dorms and listening to a band called Ozric Tentacles. I knew I wanted to try it again at larger doses and read psyche-delic literature. Timothy Leary, Robert Anton Wilson, Aleister Crowley, Clive Barker, and William S. Burroughs all gave me a vision of psychedelics that placed them in the framework of an initiatory mystic experience that could lead to a greater understanding of reality.

Around the same time that I discovered psychedelics, my father bought me Dale Carnegie's *How to Win Friends and Influence People*. I read it in a day and a half from cover to cover and loved it. I knew at that moment that I wanted to study psychology. Psychology and psychedelics both presented as potential means of escape within a few months of each other.

My reason for wanting to study psychology and what Carne-gie's book caused me to realise was: we all have a mind. If the mind is the perceptual lens through which everything is filtered, it would only be a case of cleaning that lens for everything to become clear and for project "escape from hell" to be achieved.

So I was consuming fiction, then psychology and self-help books, all with a view to "escape the dark world" or perhaps to fix it. Perhaps to offer a solution to my parents and their parents and their parents' parents all the way through the shitty ances-tral line that would make them stop acting like such dreadful arseholes.

Somewhere along the way, I ran into some articles and then some slender books on Buddhism. The attraction was instant. Buddhism identified the exact same problem that I did and presented solutions in neat formulas and aphorisms. I love formulas and aphorisms.

The fourfold formula I got from Buddhism was as follows:

1. that all of conscious life is experienced as suffering;
2. that suffering is brought about by one's attachment to unfulfilled desire;
3. that there is a practise to help us to detach from craving and desire;
4. that if you follow the "noble eightfold path of Buddhism," the detachment it brings will ultimately yield a supra state of being called "enlightenment."

Boom, all done, you're fixed, and so is the world. Who doesn't love a neat narrative with a beginning, middle, and end that presents a practical solution to our problems that we can easily grasp?

On that basis, I began to focus more on making enlightenment happen. No, I didn't know all the work, time, dedication, meditative practise, and therapy it would take to undo the traumas I had already experienced. I was fourteen. I didn't use the word trauma. I didn't know about PTSD, and I certainly would not have thought it applied to me.

I had been sexually abused in my early childhood, and I was stalked, groomed, and sexually abused again at boarding school, but I didn't know it. I didn't have the words or the concepts for that. I didn't know what was normal or acceptable or legal or criminal or moral. I was simply too young.

With my immature understanding of complex and ancient Vedic principles, I thought I had been presented with a simple formula and a simple solution: get to the Nirvana state of enlightenment and escape hell. I went all out with it as I was suffering pretty badly. Though I didn't know it at the time, my subjective life was defined by a series of cascading emotional and PTSD flashbacks. Sexual and physical abuse and boundary breaks over the years had made me very emotionally labile, and I would swing into states of dissociation, anxiety, depression, and rage rapidly. Cycling through these emotions throughout the day made normal life exhausting and painful. Psychologist and author Pia Mellody once commented that "the codependent becomes allergic to their own emotions and needs." If we accept this framework, I was constantly in an uncomfortable allergic psychic reaction of one form or another.

I tried magic; I tried hypnosis affirmations, visualisation, ceremonies, and vision boards. I tried meditation and chanting too, but progress on all counts was bewilderingly slow. In the books I had read, it all seemed so straightforward. Was I doing something wrong? Perhaps I wasn't trying hard enough?

So I came to the next malformed and erroneous conclusion: the end of suffering lies in enlightenment, and enlightenment can be accelerated through psychedelic drugs. I'm sure you can imagine which authors from the '60s and '70s I had read to be led to that hippie conclusion.

Between the ages of fifteen and eighteen, I took acid about

twelve times. Never frivolously, never for fun, and I always took notes in case I stumbled across "the secret" or "the magic formula" for my young broken heart and my, by now, quite damaged mind.

I am not a fan of people promoting psychedelics in a flippant way, and I'm afraid there are too many public intellectuals and authors who do exactly that. I know all too well how it can go very, very wrong. So let me issue a warning to anyone who is thinking of doing psychedelics: don't underestimate how intensely damaging they can be. Especially if you are carrying trauma. I'm not going to say that they cannot help—they certainly can—but they are not a shortcut to overcoming trauma. I don't care how many success stories are out there. These are powerful chemicals with powerful effects on our perceptual filters. Respect them. Be very, very careful.

I have a hypothesis about the slew of success stories and the psychedelics-are-fantastic cult that has arisen in the last twenty years or so that I'd like to share with you. It runs as follows:

If a fifty-year-old author or public intellectual who is exceptionally bright knows how to construct a narrative, is fairly mature, and lives a fairly staid middle-class life wants to have a whacky weekend away, they can probably do so in relative safety. I don't doubt it.

They can then return to normality with the "gift of fire" to impress their friends, followers, and readers alike with their insights. I think it's safe to assume that their intelligence, maturity, and capacity to construct stable narratives has done much to protect them. The people promoting the benefits of psychedelics are not emotionally dysregulated, low functioning, traumatised, or vulnerable, generally speaking. Perhaps their financial security and the stability of their normal daily life is a counterbalance to the turbulence of the psychedelic experience. Perhaps we could even say their lives are too safe, too repetitive, and the whacky weekend in the clutches of DMT, ayahuasca, or acid is exactly what they need to get out of their comfort zone.

This is not true for the traumatised person clutching on to the last scraps of reality they can by their fingertips.

And at the risk of sounding too cynical, let us not forget: the fifty-year-old author constructs stories for a living and is rewarded for "returning to the tribe" with stories of wonder, enlightenment, prophecies, and courage. I'm not saying they are liars; that would be an absurd and unjust claim.

What I am saying is: don't be naïve.

If you choose to take the drugs, please remember: when the psychedelic grips your system with its powerful and coarse hand and thrusts you into that colourful abyss, that author or public intellectual who sold you on the idea of its wonderful benefits won't be there. There will just be you. Your terror. Your despair. Your anxieties. Your pain. Your demons. Trapped in the perceptual prison with the drug itself. There is no guarantee it's going to be gentle with you.

I'm not saying, "Don't do it," either. It's your choice.

After all, who knows? If you have a great guide, plenty of therapy, plenty of meditation to ground you beforehand, a good environment in which to do it, good enough parents, and a nontraumatic childhood experience, then perhaps you won't be torn to shreds by the inner demons lurking in your shadow when you are gripped by that savage hand.

So, when considering psychedelics or promoting their use, we should all be aware and respectful of the fact that somewhere out there is an extremely damaged adolescent in terrible pain who is desperate for a way out but who doesn't know how to interpret the message. Who can't distinguish between bravado, exaggeration, and agenda. Who simply hears: "drugs are a fast track for healing and enlightenment, so take them and take them now."

In my case, I naïvely took the words of elders I would never meet who were trying to sell books and seminars, and I crashed and burned and blamed myself. And did it again. And again. And again. Surely, it must be my fault.

None of these would-be gurus would have looked the fifteen-year-old me in the eyes and told me that psychedelics were the perfect solution for my problem. I had been sexually abused. I needed therapy.

Well, in truth, all I really needed were adults who loved me and could take care of me. I needed guidance, not drugs. But I was simply left to fall by the wayside. Whose responsibility was I anyway?

No one's, apparently.

So I followed Alice all the way down the rabbit hole of LSD.

THE ACCIDENTAL YOUTUBER

It was never my intention to talk about narcissism—in my life or in others'. Personally, I didn't like the topic. My leaning was towards neurolinguistic programming, hypnotherapy, goal setting, and anything that was "forward looking." I held most practises of looking into the past as narcissistic navel-gazing with only little value but the potential to damage a person. To this day, I can still see how looking back in anger can hurt us as much as heal us, and I believe that all backward looking should be counterbalanced with just as much forward looking by planning, goal setting, establishing values, and so on in any given session. So it was not with any purpose that I became known for talking about narcissistic abuse in families, CPTSD, childhood trauma, and their effects.

In fact, it's fair to say the channel I started on YouTube came to be known for focusing on narcissistic abuse by accident. Truth be told I had been in relationships that, by any measure, would tick the boxes for narcissistic abuse. But I remember looking for help online many, many years ago only to be appalled by what I saw in the online narcissistic abuse forums and the entirely toxic culture of the self-appointed, so-called "empaths" to be found there. The posturing, the doxing of exes, the echo chamber, the unquestioning acceptance that what people perceived to be true about their ex-partners couldn't possibly be considered anything other than toxic cesspools of covert narcissism.

The quote by Ralph Waldo Emerson came to mind: "The more he spoke of his honour, the faster we counted our spoons." The more aggressively and passionately these people expressed their victimhood status and how awfully their exes had treated them to strangers online, the more I wondered who the real victim was.

So how did I come to start a channel with now over 300,000 followers and 37 million views on a subject I had relatively little knowledge of and little interest in at the channel's inception?

Well, that all comes down to the daughters of narcissistic mothers, oddly enough, as, you may have guessed, I do not count myself among them.

Permit me a brief history of my time working online.

Back in 2001, I was waiting to see whether I could or would join the army as an officer. If it didn't work out, I was considering the police force as a second option on the graduate fast track scheme they had running.

Though serious about both options, I had the sense that no matter what happened with the army or the police, I wanted an online side business to generate this mythical (and oh, is it ever a mythical beast) thing called "passive income." Or at least to understand how online businesses worked. The allure of setting up a machine that would accumulate money while I did nothing was great. These were the early days; I was naïve but very impressed by the promises of the various gurus who were teaching online marketing back in the year 2000.

However, at that time I didn't even have an email address, and my typing was of the "hunt and peck" variety. I acquired a course by a Canadian chap called Corey Rudl on setting up an online business, and I followed his advice to the letter. I set up a YouTube channel and a website that sold self-defence material that I created with my friends in my living room or in local gyms. It included DVDs, audio hypnoses, and e-books. My interest and the selling point that made me stand out in the market was an emphasis on the psychological and emotional elements of martial arts training.

It went slowly at first, but because my ambitions were small, I was happy with it. If it gave me enough money to put fuel in the car and buy food for the week, that was enough for me. I was running this business in my twenties whilst doing other things and waiting to see how my applications with the army and the police force went. I was also doing other jobs: nightclub security, gym work, taxiing, and then ultimately working in the UK school system. It was very much a side hustle.

At first.

Eventually it started to blossom and became my full-time work. Over time, as the brand grew and my reputation for teaching the psychology of combatives flourished, I got access to more and more qualified professionals internationally (but mainly in America) in law enforcement, private security, the military, and so on. I developed closer bonds with guys who were, by all standards, pretty tough chaps—many of them skilled operators, some pro fighters, and a good number of the martial arts instructors themselves.

They knew I had that nefarious thing called "a background in psychology," and so some of them would ask me more and more questions relating to their personal lives and relationships as trust between us grew. Questions were less about training students to access aggression under stressful situations and more about how to negotiate time visited with children and ex-wives.

Over time, I decided to turn this into a separate venture where I would offer life coaching specifically to martial arts/LEO/combatives instructors on any and every element of their personal and emotional lives.

As I put more and more focus onto helping this primarily male base to navigate the chaotic waters in their lives, I noticed certain recurring themes coming up time and time again. These were all to do with weak boundaries and, counterintuitively, a seeming inability to assert themselves. Obviously most of these men were perfectly capable of asserting their boundaries in a professional context (for some of them, a tested boundary would result in them shooting the boundary-pusher dead), but these same men would struggle to show that level of confidence and decisiveness in other contexts in their lives.

And these contexts would always be intimate. With wives, girl-friends, children, and family members, the lines for these men got blurry. They were loyal, duty-bound, and good samurai who showed their love through sacrifice. This often seemed to lead to them getting their asses handed to them by people who did not reciprocate the same values of loyalty and honour.

In Japanese, samurai translates (roughly) to "one who serves their master." The tendency among these loyal men who valued duty very highly was to respond with obedience to top-down authority and to be able to assert top-down authority themselves and command obedience in a well-defined hierarchy.

The problem was that outside of well-defined hierarchies, they tended to conflate blind subservience with loyalty where the "rules of engagement" were either unclear or shifting.

This topic area was all new to me; I claimed no expertise or authority. However, I shared with them that I had suffered from the same confusion and vulnerability. Because I understood their communication style, we could meaningfully engage in a conversational exploration of the core issues.

I promised them nothing. No guaranteed results, no working systemic solution to overcome the problem, only a sympathetic, nonjudgmental ear and the promise that I would study the issues they raised and try to work towards developing new solutions.

From this I started a new YouTube channel and concept called "Spartanlifecoach." The focus was initially on helping instructors, pro fighters, law enforcement, military, and MMA coaches to assert their boundaries and overcome this thing I was calling people-pleaser syndrome.

Through these conversations and my research, I noted fifteen common traits of people-pleaser syndrome. Note that this concept is a gateway to my conceptualisation of Echo Codependency but is not a precursor model per se.

The fifteen traits of people pleasers:

1. emotophobia: fear of negative emotions; never wanting anybody to feel bad
2. neurotic levels of naïveté (denial)

3. neurotic desire to be liked and addiction to attention, even negative
4. external locus of control (relying on outside permission)
5. inability to say "no" (boundaries), especially if there is the use of guilting, shaming, whining, or any form of emotional blackmailing
6. excessive conscientiousness (taking as little space as possible because of lack of self-worth)
7. blurry sense of self (no boundaries), feeling other people's emotions and thoughts
8. emotional dependence (codependence): after abuse, some self-isolation (avoidance) and continuously playing the abuse from within—but two make perfect romantic wound-mates, closed together tightly
9. low self-confidence, low self-worth (having been treated like a piece of shit and believing it)
10. overintellectualisation, rationalisation, and justification of the abusive situation
11. being addicted to approval
12. emotional immaturity
13. too altruistic and compassionate, neurotically wanting to help or keep everybody happy all the time
14. loneliness, isolation (becoming a beggar)
15. easily impressed by new concepts, things, and people

This became the starting point for the "Spartanlifecoach" YouTube channel.

Once the videos were up and the conversation was started online, it wasn't long before I was drawn into studying narcissistic abuse as a means of analysing the ways in which one person in a relationship can feel like they are perpetually on the losing side and like their partner is exploiting them.

I read the DSM (*Diagnostic and Statistical Manual of Mental Disorders*) definitions, purchased a JSTOR (journal storage) account, and read some papers pertinent to narcissistic personality disorder.

The interest in my little YouTube channel skyrocketed once I started talking about narcissism. The video that really pushed the channel forward was called "The daughters of narcissistic abuse." Obviously I had to read up on the subject in order to make the video.

My style of developing courses and content has always been conversational. I chat to the market and let people tell me what it is they are interested in and what they want rather than choosing for them what it is I believe they should know. In an online conversation about narcissism, there was a surge of interest around a comment from the daughter of a narcissistic mother, so I decided to address the issue in a video. I had accidentally hit a wave of interest in narcissism at just the right moment.

Though not the daughter of a narcissistic mother myself, in order to answer the question from a female friend, I did a Google search and found a site called daughtersofnarcissisticmothers.com. This contained articles on two topics, which I then raised in a video that, back in 2014, had not had much attention on YouTube. The first was "splitting," in which the traumatised person engages in "black and white" thinking. In the case of a narcissistic mother, it can lead them to think of a daughter as "all good" or "all bad."

This naturally led to the second topic of interest, "the golden child and the scapegoat/black sheep." The mother who engages in splitting may end up seeing one child as the embodiment of good who can do no wrong in her eyes, also known as "the golden child." Another child may then be viewed as altogether bad, one who cannot do anything right in the eyes of the mother. Many people recognised the process of splitting in their relationships with narcissists and also their place as "scapegoat" or "black sheep" within the family unit. This resonated so strongly with people that I had unknowingly created my first viral video.

It also led me, begrudgingly, to have more respect for narcissism as a subject and the more "backward looking" therapeutic modalities. As I was studying and developing courses to help others, it caused me to explore my own relationships with former partners, family members, and friends through the lens of narcissism and narcissistic abuse. I realised there has been far more of it in my life than I'd previously known.

One of the major watershed moments in developing my understanding of the topic came when I was led to the concept of CPTSD as described by Pete Walker in his excellent book *Complex PTSD: From Surviving to Thriving*. I felt, reading his book, like I had found some sort of holy grail. So many pieces of the puzzle fell into place so clearly and completely for me. No other single book has had such a deep impact on my view of psychology or healing as a whole.

Along my journey, I began to explore certain concepts and

terms that were key to my development of the Echo Codependency model.

NPD was first identified by psychoanalyst Heinz Kohut in 1967. It was seen as excessive self-admiration rooted in a failure to develop feelings of love outwards in childhood. The internalisation of feelings of love more appropriately given for others being directed towards the self was seen as failure to develop from the natural and healthy developmental stage of megalomania and narcissism we all pass through in childhood. It was previously identified as a destructive form of self-obsession by Freud and others. The inspiration for the name "narcissistic" comes from Ovid's tale of the beautiful young hunter Narcissus, who, rejecting the attention of all who loved him, including the wood nymph Echo, is cursed to fall in love with his own reflection. He then withers away unto death, unable to tear his gaze away from his own self.

CPTSD was identified by professor Judith Hermann in 1992. As opposed to standard PTSD, which is typically associated with singular events and more easily identifiable responses to key triggers, complex trauma is typically associated with circumstances the client could not escape where multiple stressors across multiple vulnerabilities were experienced in a way much more difficult for the client to identify. The cause of trauma is complex. And the symptoms of the trauma are more complex, too. Emotional dysregulation, a shaky sense of self, and hypervigilance about a world perceived to be very dangerous are all present. Present, too, are "emotional flashbacks," where emotions from previous traumatic experiences are unknowingly triggered and the sufferer feels intense negative emotions without knowing their cause.

Narcissistic abuse was identified by professor Sam Vaknin in 1995. Vaknin writes,

> In 1995, I coined the phrase 'narcissistic abuse' to describe a subtype of abusive behavior that was all-pervasive (across multiple areas of life) and involved a plethora of behaviors and manipulative or coercive techniques. Narcissistic abuse differed from all other types of abuse in its range, sophistication, duration, versatility, and expression, and premeditated intention to negate and vitiate the victim's personal autonomy, agency, self-efficacy, and wellbeing.

Over the years, as I explored narcissistic abuse and how to help people recover from it through the lens of Pete Walker's CPTSD model, I found my perception of psychological issues undergoing a major shift. It became clearer to me just how much of the suffering people ascribe to their emotional and mental states is caused by trauma and learned survival responses to that trauma. We'll go a little deeper into these survival responses that unconsciously affect so much of our lives in a later chapter.

From here, I developed a more extensive definition of codependency as a whole way of being (or rather "not being") as a learned survival response in the face of harsh traumatic conditions.

Effectively, what I'm calling Echo Codependency is a mirror image of what we commonly call narcissism. This is the Echo to Narcissus or the response to the wounding. The yin to the narcissist's yang. The ultimate apex predator meets the ultimate prey.

Which was what I had become in my intimate relationships.

CHAPTER 4

IN LOVE AND WAR

MY DREAMS WERE SHATTERED ALL AT ONCE.

It was 3:00 a.m., and I was deep asleep in pitch blackness. What had torn this dark calm so catastrophically was the sound of someone screaming and swearing at me. Flecks of spit were hitting my face as a stream of incomprehensible vitriol was poured over my head. This was perhaps the fifth such incident that month.

I had moved from the UK to Dublin to rescue Salome, my ex-girlfriend, who had gotten herself and her dog kicked out of the shared house she was in and could not find anywhere else to live. Dublin is very expensive, and the landlords have so many choices that they don't need to accept dogs. Salome had chosen to do a job that she loved for very little money in a very expensive city, and she was in trouble. Hence the need for my rescue.

Rescuing people, but particularly my intimate partners, is

something I've done my whole life. It's a neurotic compulsion to play a role in a psychodrama that does no one any good. Yet I seem to be stuck on repeat: try, try, and try again.

As my not-very-grateful rescued ex stood over me and screamed in the night, my sluggish thoughts struggled to defend against this invasion, and I realised that she was already deep in the middle of an argument with me. It seemed I was losing.

This clearly had not started when she walked in the room. Obviously, she had been awake, arguing in her head with me, pacing the living room, no doubt, and then had burst into the bedroom and begun screaming at the real me, rather than just her internalised avatar of me, as her delusion overlapped into reality.

"...and you need to fucking learn! And I'm not fucking telling you again! You get this sorted out right fucking now, or we are done!" And so on.

I opened my eyes and said as calmly as I could, "Go to the living room, and we'll talk about this. You'll wake up the neighbours. Go on."

I have a distinct, crisp memory of putting on a shirt. I never wear a shirt. It was 3:00 a.m., I could have gone in a vest. But, no, I sat on the bed, staring straight ahead, buttoning up my shirt like a man readying himself for an early-morning firing squad.

We had been at our own Balrog–Gandalf death struggle for the best part of three years. As we reached the terminus, the battles were getting more and more desperate.

Salome was very and blatantly sick. I'm not a qualified clinician, but I spoke to some who gave me all the feedback they could. One counsellor laughed when he found I was a public speaker on the subject of narcissistic abuse. He said to me, "Well, seeing as you're such an expert, if she's not got narcissistic personality disorder, then who does?"

The counsellor had made a good point. A bomb of a point. A bomb that went off and destroyed the layers and layers of denial I'd built around my desire to keep the relationship going. Why did I want to keep it going? I was being used and abused daily, yet I still felt compelled to fix everything. Almost as though I felt my abuse was my fault.

Daily life with Salome was frustrating and exhausting. Nothing I ever did seemed to be right. She didn't always tell me I was a disappointment to her, but through metacommunication (body language, facial expression, and voice tone) the message was delivered loudly, frequently, and clearly: you are not good enough.

Then there were the constant traps. I would be led into conversational cul-de-sacs that had booby traps built into them many times a day. The protocol would be as follows:

1. Be led into a conversation about a topic I had no interest in.
2. Be bullied with questions about said topic in an aggressive interrogation style.
3. Eventually be pushed into whatever trip wire was built into the conversation. "Oh, so you're saying you basically hate women then!"

4. Ambient emotional abuse would follow. (Ambient abuse is generally categorised as a stealthy, insidious form of abuse that cultivates an atmosphere of fear/irritation.) Salome would sulk and behave as though I had wronged her in the most critical ways.

5. There was no way out as talking about it would be taken as further hateful actions initiated by me.

6. This would lead to me "walking on eggshells" to avoid the trip wires as her persecutory self-pitying sulking could go on for hours and occasionally days.

Then there was the constant talk about other men. Ex-boyfriends, men she had known, men she worked with, men she met at the shop. This often boring tirade of jealousy-inducing white noise hurt me on two levels. It made me feel both insecure and stupid for falling prey to such an adolescent tactic.

In addition to this, I faced at least two "tests" a day. These could be tests of my manhood—"Are you strong enough?"—tests of my love for her—"Do you love me enough?"—or tests of my knowledge of her background, tastes, and preferences—"Do you care enough to know whether I prefer mustard or tomato sauce on a hot dog?"

This last example is not a joke. Three months into our relationship, she went berserk, shook with rage, and then had a hysterical crying fit for thirty minutes because I "forgot" (I swear by Christ and all the saints I had never had the required data to forget it) that she could not stand mustard on hot dogs! Mustard was for dogs! Decadents! Monsters! And those who thought genocide a fine way to spend an afternoon.

I was also berated for two days for failing to remember her favourite flavour of Fanta (I'll confess to perhaps having known but not giving it the appropriate level of urgent attention and informing the UN as I should have). Later that same month, we stayed at my friend's house for New Year's Eve, but we did not sleep all night as she was literally shaking with rage that I had momentarily forgotten her Chinese astrological sign. Then she wept hysterically.

The effects on me were deleterious. I was constantly anxious and depressed. I developed a powerful case of insomnia where I would snap awake at 4:00 a.m., chest pounding, dreaming of intense violence, unable to go back to sleep for hours. I gained about ten kilograms in six months, and I started to become very vulnerable to any and all colds or coughs going around, which was not like me.

Why did you not leave? Any sane person would ask it.

I tried.

At the four-month point, I packed my things to leave and had the chat with her.

She knelt on the ground sobbing and begging and swearing she would change. She would get help. Seek out a therapist. She knew she was doing it, but she couldn't stop.

She leaned heavily on the fact that I was aware she had escaped a genocide in the '90s and had moved to Sweden and lived as a refugee. Aside from experiencing her family members killed for their ethnicity back home, she was then bullied in Sweden for hers.

This was another area of the relationship that was tough for me. She was utterly obsessed with race and detecting people's nationality and ethnicity by looking at them. I'm a liberal Englishman with a degree in psychology who leans left of centre, and this kind of thing is way outside of my cultural boundaries and made me uncomfortable.

She would, at monthly intervals, try to force me to play a game with her where we would guess people's races or nationalities by looking at them. I told her time and again I did not want to play this game, but she would persist.

"Oh, come ooooon, don't be such a baby. Just tell me: do you think this woman is Russian or Chechen?"

"I don't know. And I don't care. Please stop."

"Oh, come ooooooooooon, just say it. Russian or Chechen?" She would become lighthearted and jovial as though it were just a silly game of no import.

"Okay, she's Chechen. Can we go now please?"

"Why? Why? Why did you say that? Are you a fucking idiot? She's clearly Russian."

Then there would be a rage-fuelled diatribe about Russian facial features that I didn't and don't particularly care about. In her eyes the message was simple: "You have failed again. Idiot."

Because I was a good, understanding man with a background in psychology who'd been trained not to judge people morally and to see everyone as just "victims of victims," I let myself be consumed by this intensely mentally unwell woman again and again.

"It's not her fault. She escaped a genocide. She just has PTSD. She said she will go to a therapist next week. She promised she would change."

Having convinced me to give her one last chance, do you think she went to a therapist? Do you think she changed?

I'm ashamed to say I let this cycle of leaving, begging, promising, and staying play out six times before I finally got the courage to leave.

By the time I did, my confidence was completely shredded, and my ability to even see reality as it was had taken several blows too.

When the counsellor in Dublin confronted me with the reasonable question "If not her, then who?" I felt like a hypocrite. Here is a synopsis of the reasoning I used with myself to get out of denial:

1. NPD exists and is meaningful as a diagnosis, or it isn't.
2. If it isn't, tell everyone now that this is what you believe and close your YouTube channel.
3. If it exists in a meaningful diagnostic sense and is discrete from other issues (autism, brain damage, PTSD, etc.), then it has a series of detectable traits.
4. You either agree with the traits laid out in mainstream psychiatry or you don't. If you agree, then you know the traits. You know perfectly well if she exhibits them or not.

5. Your girlfriend is not Schrödinger's girlfriend. She either fits the bill for the diagnostic criteria or she does not. She is not "in both realities equally weighted as the same thing until the box opens."

This was my dead end as far as the relationship went. The death of hope, the moment of despair, and the beginning of my grieving process.

Am I stating in writing that my ex absolutely had NPD? No, I'm not. I couldn't possibly do that. But if you read what I just wrote carefully, you will see: there are traits that are either there or are not.

If you can see a consistent pattern of more than six of the following, it's time to stop kidding yourself and accept that your partner is at least an irredeemable shit if not an actual clinical malignant narcissist:

- excessive need for admiration
- bullying, exploitative interpersonal style
- vindictive
- entitled
- belief in their own specialness
- extremely envious
- obsessed with a fantasy-based version of themselves
- lacking empathy
- massive arrogance

I loved Salome. I really did. I was loyal to her and thought the world of her. But neither of us could stop the monster inside of her, nor could our relationship survive its infrastructure-destroying cycles of misbehaviour. She was sweet and kind in public and a monstrous, sadistic, delusional bully in private.

So now—why did I put up with it? Why does anyone put up with blatant mistreatment?

The classic psychology line of reasoning will broadly say something like: "If you learned that love was abusive in childhood, then having an abusive lover will feel a lot like home in adulthood." In other words, we are inculcated or hypernormalised to abusive patterns of love and intimacy. It's the water we aren't even aware we are swimming in, so we have no way of developing an awareness of its existence. This, however, is a crucial but partial telling of the truth about why we, who have experienced this kind of narcissistic abuse, stay.

Yes, we microcosmically have our individual traumas and problems, this is true, but I think there are broader macrocosmic problems at the cultural level here, too.

What I've observed over the last twenty-five years of dating is a subtle but strong shift in attitudes toward partners and love itself. It's become much more aggressive. When listening to conversations or reading articles on the subject, we can see that the language around love, intimacy, and sex is quite cold and savage.

I remember someone I know very well once told me that "love is a game of winners and losers." This seems like a very sad outlook to me, but since she said that to me over a decade ago, it's almost as though the majority of people have internalised this belief. The relationship I described above that eventually terminated was a classic example of that.

Salome's stance towards me was combative from the outset. When I was with her, I truly felt that she saw me as an enemy to be duped and conquered. When I challenged her with this observation, she denied it. "I love you; you know I love you with all my heart; I would never see someone I love like that."

This is another thing I've observed: people claiming to love the other person as a shield to any potential criticism of bad, boundary-breaking, disrespectful behaviour and as a get-out-of-jail-free card. As though, "But I love you" means, "Therefore I can do no wrong" or "Therefore all wrongdoing must be forgiven."

I've also been told by my last three girlfriends, all of whom I had terrible problems with over their pathological lying, "If you love me you should trust me; I would never lie to you." This within minutes of confronting them with evidence that they had, indeed, recently lied to me.

So what is happening here? Are we training people to see love and sex as a form of combat between two opposing teams? Are there really just winners and losers? If so, what does it take to win in the modern dating domain?

I'm not advocating you try to "win." Instead, I'm going to try to demonstrate why such attitudes and behaviours follow in the footsteps of adopting a consumer's mindset.

The advice offered by modern dating coaches of both sexes runs as follows: "The power in the relationship lies with the one who needs the relationship the least." Well, if that's true, you must keep all your options open at all times and never fully commit. You should also try to lure your opponent into committing more than you are committing so that you can "stay in control." Maybe try tricking them into investing in you financially or promising things in the future you have no intention of delivering so that they emotionally invest whilst you coolly sit back and watch their attempts to please you?

Does all this sound familiar?

I cannot say for certain, but I'm tempted to wonder if consumer capitalism hasn't truly rotted our minds at this point. Do we now see love, sex, and relationships as commodities to be consumed?

That would mean we would adopt a consumer's mindset: people are not people but options (like your favourite brand of car or clothes). They are not people but services and products. Love is no longer love but a consumer paying for the services rendered with time, attention, affection, and sex.

How disappointed do people get when it doesn't work out exactly as they wished it would? I sometimes detect the same infantile frustration people can go into when the product they paid for doesn't work quite the way it should. Or when the five-star holiday didn't live up to expectations. There is a blustering indignation—yes, I've heard it in myself too—that smacks of "demanding to see the manager."

We need to put the vehicle in reverse. Nowhere do we need to be more emotionally mature, grounded, careful, conscious, and boundaried than in our intimate relationships. Intimacy always leads to shadow activation in both yourself and the other. This means you are going to spew up some ugly stuff you didn't know was there, and so are they. This, ironically, is a sign of increased intimacy. The closer you get, the more you will be triggered, and so will they.

If we can get intimacy, love, and sex right, our lives can be heavenly. If we get them wrong—and so many, many do—it becomes hell on earth. If you're not careful, you will witness your partner change into a demon before your very eyes.

Why? Consumer capitalism teaches us greed and immaturity. Because consumer capitalism preys on and leverages human weakness to compel us to buy things we want instead of only buying the things we need, it naturally and unintentionally creates "shadow activation." If we want to dilate people's wants so that they want more and buy more, it means we must provoke their selfishness, greed, and envy. Within such a culture, when it comes time for intimacy, the populace who are already shadow activated and trained to be entitled, impulsive, and self-indulgent have a very hard time maintaining interpersonal boundaries. All the unconscious "stuff," including unresolved traumas from ex-girlfriends and -boyfriends, will come bubbling out and land on you, and you will spew your stuff onto your partner, too.

The idea we have now in modern culture that sex isn't psychologically risky, that bonds can be formed and broken at will with no cost, and that promiscuity is a sensible way to run our lives is really very dangerous.

These are powerful instincts we are provoking in ourselves and others. Some of the MOST powerful known to humanity, and they are not to be taken lightly. Don't be surprised when the divorces and the breakups you see around you get nasty. People, generally speaking, don't have the internal infrastructure to stop that from happening. And don't be surprised if you struggle to keep relationships afloat for long either. In all likelihood, neither you nor the person you are with has the proper training for such an endeavour as two adults cohabitating across time in a loving and supportive way.

I know you don't have such training, and neither do I because it doesn't exist—but it should! The world is lacking in real love and real intimacy. Real intimacy requires vulnerability. Real vulnerability can only be done safely by people with strong boundaries, interacting with others with good boundaries within a boundaried environment.

Sorry if this sounds like a lecture, but I think it's a key element of the Echo Codependency puzzle: we must have rules of engagement, and we must all stick to them. In an environment of pure permissive chaos, of course predators will take over, win, hurt everyone else, and lead their victims to act like the predators who hurt them.

A narcissistic demon scratches and hurts a human with its poisoned talons. That human may choose, in their pain, to act demonically for a while and go on to scratch five more people. The replication rate of this virus becomes five and spreads quickly into a pandemic of hurt people who hurt people.

What can stop this?

We need to sit back and take a breath from the hysterical

surge toward the future and all the weight of intergenerational trauma that shoves us forward violently from behind us. We must step out, detach, take no action, cause no ripples, and generate no further karma for a while.

Seek therapy, get over your exes, get over what your parents did to you, or at least acknowledge it. Go to therapy with your partner, talk, be vulnerable, respect each other. You will still have days where the demons win and you project your shadow onto your partner, but if you are both alert and compassionate, I expect those days will be less and less frequent. Try: "This is your shadow activation, my love. I choose not to respond to what you are saying right now." Echo Codependency will only flourish in an environment where it is not safe to love and nurture the other safely and respectfully.

If you are in a safe, loving, respectful relationship right now, I salute you.

From the rest of us: it's a bloody war zone out here!

CHAPTER 5

BUILDING BETTER BOUNDARIES

WHEN I WAS TWENTY-NINE, I MET A GIRL. SHE WAS EVERYTHING I could have hoped for and more. It was wonderful. It ruined my life.

The pain and destruction of an abusive relationship can last a worryingly long time. Depending on the type of abuse experienced, it can lead to a "wound that refuses to heal."

In this case, the relationship started well enough. Wu and I had known each other for seven years through gym and martial arts training and had reconnected through Facebook. On the first night that we decided to go out together, we ended up in bed.

This was somewhat predictable as we had been physically intimate before. She was a gymnast. I was working as a gym instructor and teaching Muay Thai for extra cash in between doing nightclub security, tending bar, and doing various other bits and pieces. I think our relationship started that first time when I began giving her martial arts training. It hadn't lasted long. We'd split up after a few months because she couldn't keep her hands off my friends.

That was our history up to that point. We got on really well, had the same stupid sense of humour and a love of going out and partying, and the sexual connection was very, very strong.

At that time, at age twenty-nine, I was teaching self-defence full time, and business was doing really well. Back in 2008, despite the economic collapse, the interest in seminars and courses was very strong. I was busy, I had a good business, things were going well, I was enjoying training, and then this great girl reentered my life.

It was great. At first.

The problems came when two specific factors entered the scenario: alcohol and men.

I did my best to ignore the fact that Wu was actively eye-fucking every guy in the room because I knew acknowledgement would lead to the termination of the relationship. It wasn't even an argument I wanted to have. Once alcohol was added, the flirtation moved up from eye contact and smiling to chatting, dancing, and a little light touching. If cocaine was sprinkled in, then sometimes that could calm her down and bring her back to some semblance of a boundary. Sometimes.

So after maybe three months of holding my tongue, and following a particularly egregious night out with her standing in a group of men, showing off in front of her friends, I left the club in a drunken fury. What followed was a typical dignity-destroying, alcohol- and jealousy-infused 3:00 a.m. ego-wrestling match over whose fault the scenario was.

I should have left her. I did not leave her. I lost a little more of my self-respect.

A word here about boundaries and setting them. A boundary is not set with a word. Telling people you have a boundary is merely to notice that they are approaching it. But it is not setting one.

The setting of a boundary requires a consequence, and a consequence requires an action. Words are not actions but merely the promise of them. Boundary setting also requires some kind of a sacrifice. Why? Well, because the setting of a boundary, by definition, is outside the comfort zone.

We as human beings have evolved, generally speaking, to be cooperative. It's an imperative for our survival to work with others and to join forces and skills in line with common goals. To this end, we sacrifice our individual wants and idiosyncrasies in order to conform to group norms and to the culture of our tribe.

In psychology, the personality trait pertinent to cooperativeness is called "agreeableness." People high in agreeableness tend to "agree" more and be more conflict-averse. This makes them more friendly and more polite, which makes them seem more empathic.

The problem with a person who falls prey to the temptation

to be "hyperagreeable"—and it is a temptation to be resisted—
is that they get walked all over. They are ever at the behest of
people and situations to fulfil the needs and demands of others
and to mould their intent with perfect plasticity to whatever
comes their way.

If what comes their way is good, life-affirming, healthy, and
in their best interests, then that is fine. Generally speaking,
though, when bobbing along the chaotic tides of this reality,
how much random flotsam that pings our radars is incidentally
good, life-affirming, and healthy? I would venture: relatively
little.

It behoves us to plot a course and then work hard towards not
being blown off that course, knowing that, with every day that
passes, a multitude of things, events, and people will show up
doing exactly that—looking like the fat-cheeked cherubim who
lean down from the sky and blow boats around in those old
maritime maps.

It's more comfortable to simply say "yes." No one will be angry
with you if you just say "yes." You won't be judged or shunned
if you simply do as you are told.

Anyway, on top of one's genetic proclivity to agreeableness, isn't
that what school trains us to do from a very young age? Sit down,
shut up, sit still. Naughty children are disobedient. Good children are subservient to the will of the big other.

If you tell someone, "If you keep doing this thing I don't like,
then there will be a consequence," but no consequence appears,
you're essentially telling them, "I may sound off a bit about

the thing you're doing, but I'm powerless to stop you. So keep on going." Action X must lead to consequence Y, or it's not a boundary.

A word now about strong versus weak boundaries. A weak consequence (like expressing your displeasure with your partner by sulking or giving them the silent treatment) is as toxic to the relationship and as manipulative as the abusive behaviour it is intended to coerce.

Boundaries work best as openly, cheerfully, and energetically expressed expectations based on a sound moral philosophy. "I'm afraid I just can't have someone in my life who does X. The consequence of that, both for me and for you, must be Y." It should be expressed almost as though there is nothing you can do about it. Which, in truth, you can't. If your boundaries are real and strong, they are based on such clear moral absolutes that there is nothing you, as the holder of that moral philosophy, could do to stop it!

Imagine a terrible thing a partner could do that would cause you to be rid of them no matter what. Something really awful. Let's say deliberately hurting children. Can you take your mind there? Most likely you can, and that means you actually do have a moral philosophy based on moral absolutes that you are powerless to do anything about. It's just that it's so weak and floppy from lack of use that the person would only actually cross the threshold by doing something so awful that it's universally agreed to be awful. If you knew your partner regularly hurt children and you allowed them to continue being intimate with you, you would effectively share in their culpability to a degree by letting them believe the action was acceptable.

That's very far over on the extreme side of the map of "bad things a person can do." Imagine taking that boundary and bringing it closer. Less bad things. Maybe they don't hurt children, but they hurt you. Were you not a child once? In some religious, spiritual, and psychological sense, are you not still a child now? Did you consent to this abuse? Does it make you feel awful? Can we begin to align the idea that a person hurting children is not totally unlike a person breaking our heart or crushing our dreams or humiliating us publicly again and again?

You don't lack boundaries. And I can't give you boundaries. No one can. You lack a strong moral philosophy that allows you to cheerfully and energetically declare, "That behaviour right there? That's wrong! I don't have any of that in my life. Not now, not ever. I don't care how pretty you are, what the benefits to me are, how rich you are, what access you give me, or whatever the payoff is, it's just a hard no. I'm not having it."

Then the sacrifice: you lose something when you set the boundary.

A nation that sets a hard boundary and goes to war when it's crossed loses time, money, and the lives of its citizens. It's tragic and costly, so why do we do it? Presumably because the failure to set the boundary would be more costly than simply setting it and making the sacrifice.

A boyfriend who loses the beautiful, funny, high-energy girlfriend he loves when he separates from her condemns himself to months of heartache, if not years. That's quite a toll. Are you prepared to pay it? If the answer is no, then I've just given you an explanation as to why you can't set boundaries: you aren't willing to pay the price of setting them.

Boundaries occur spontaneously when you value something or someone. They are not given or trained. You can only train someone to have the moral philosophy to value themselves (their time, attention, love, kindness, etc.) more so that they naturally set the protective boundary wall around the things they value. The valued thing must include themselves and what they offer. If you don't value yourself, your time, and your attention, well, then you're hardly going to set boundaries and make sacrifices to protect these things, are you?

That's how it was for me. I felt unlovable and generally useless. I was good at making money. I was good at teaching and motivating others, but internally I didn't feel much self-worth, especially in the areas pertinent to intimacy. Another hangover from childhood neglect and abuse: the way we love ourselves is a mirror image of how our parents loved us.

I felt "so lucky" to be with someone that, even though she was emotionally stunted, histrionic, obsessed with sex and attention, and had been abandoned by her birth father, I let her get away with things. I mean, I complained, I raged, I wept, I pled, and she would promise to change and to stop and so on. But really, why should she?

Then the inevitable happened: Wu went away without me on a hen weekend for five days, and when she came back home, she left her Facebook open to the messages she had sent to the guy she met on the hen weekend.

I'd like to tell you I split up with her straightaway, but she begged and sobbed and pled—I carried on with her for another increasingly bitter and foolish nine months. The split, when it came, was of course extremely acrimonious. I loathed her in the end. And I hated myself more for wasting more time with her.

This is not a poison pen effort. I genuinely believe that there is nothing intrinsically wrong in Wu's soul that couldn't be overcome with humility, maturity, accumulated pain, and disappointment (we all realise life isn't a big party as we get past thirty). Though we haven't spoken in eleven years, I wish her well.

One demon we must overcome in order to recover from child-hood trauma, abusive relationships, CPTSD, and codependency is a weak morality. Many of us carry a very fragile and mal-formed moral code. I know, I know, the word morality puts an awful lot of people off, but look at it this way. If we have a very weak sense of what is good versus what is bad, how will we know when to recognize and embrace the good and when to recognize and reject the bad?

At this moment in human history, our value systems and our moralities are so intensely corrupted. One of the reasons why people are so stressed out, so isolated, and so wounded is because we have no moral sense of how we should act, what to embrace, and what to reject. Like the cell wall that has been broken in the single-celled amoeba, instead of only absorbing nutrients and letting out waste, we start letting out nutrients and letting in waste. We don't recognize what's toxic because what's toxic is now so thoroughly mixed in with what we experience as the ideology of our culture.

The concept of junk values was coined by a journalist called Johann Hari. He posited the idea that we live in a time where what is put on a pedestal and what is put up as a value is no longer; in fact, they are antivalues. True values—truth, dignity, and courage—are discarded with contempt in our time. In their place are now junk values: consumerism, pleasure, promiscuity, and narcissism.

I am not a preacher; I'm not a dogmatic man; I'm not anti-pleasure; I'm not antihedonism. I suspect that, for some personalities, being utterly hedonistic from time to time is probably critical to the maintenance of that human being's sanity. However, that's not what we're talking about. We're talking about a culture that thinks it's time to party, consume, and pleasure ourselves 24/7 to such a ridiculous, extreme extent that we actually experience anxiety if we are not having enough fun. You've heard of the phenomenon of FOMO, the fear of missing out. We are so terrified that something good may be happening in a place where we are not and that we're not recording it on our phones to celebrate it on social media that we have an actual term for it. It is, to be clear, fundamentally fear. We experience a kind of terror that we've missed an opportunity to consume and to posture. I don't want to sound like my grandfather. However, I'm aware that sometimes I do.

As I say, I myself like the pleasures of the material world. I like hedonism. I like to drink; I like to dance; I like to party; I love it. But I have boundaries with that pleasure. I'm aware that if I subsumed myself in that world and only sought to pleasure myself as much as I possibly could, I would get very, very sick. I would feel unstable, my sense of purpose would diminish, and I would become mentally ill. I would experience emotional dysregulation, anxiety, and depression, and I would become, over time, quite distressed. Why is this?

The easiest and most straightforward hypothesis (yes, it has flaws, but it's a good starting point) is simply that we are not evolved for this. To actually experience a degree of choice, excess, and pleasure we have never before known in human history is a kind of stress for us. And not a minor one! We feel guilty that we're not enjoying ourselves enough. We feel ashamed that we can't just pleasure and pleasure and pleasure ourselves. We don't know what to do with the fact that it has become boring—that we've become numb—that the pleasure we're pursuing is no longer giving us the thrill that it used to. But we keep the pantomime going. After all, what else is there?

My suggested antidote to this problem is to ask people to develop their own value systems, their own morality. Not so that they become boring, stiff, and judgmental. That would be a catastrophe. But it's a real risk, and we must acknowledge it. The people who are obsessed with morality, obsessed with virtue, obsessed with discipline become the type of people who we really wouldn't want to have next to us at a dinner party or to share a drink with at the bar. You don't want to become that person either! They can become preachy, judgmental, rigid, and dogmatic, and being with them is like receiving a series of lectures.

So what do I propose? Rather than creating moralistic prudes, I'm actually just talking about helping people to be somewhat more boundaried. We can only have boundaries around things that we actually value, and we can only actually value things if we have a value system.

Most likely if you have kids or you have kids in your family, if you're a sane, seminormal person, you value them. In your value system, you find them to be lovable, cute, worthwhile, fun to spend time with, and rewarding, and you're glad that they exist in the world. Therefore, whether you know it or not, you are boundaried with them in relation to the value you assign them. If somebody tried to do something to either your own children or the children in your family if you don't have your own children, you probably would respond very aggressively and very violently. For example, if somebody tried to hurt them or kidnap them. That is an indication of an authentic, natural, unconscious boundary that is around something that you already value. You don't need to learn how to assert boundaries; it's not necessary, and it's actually quite awkward.

When people try to adopt exogenous boundaries, they tend to look a bit goofy. It all feels a bit fake and forced. They start to confuse pushiness and hostility with assertiveness and honesty. Why? Because they're playing a fake game, which is what happens when we have taken our boundaries from outside. There is another way, a better way: from the inside out. Or, in other words, raising the value you have on yourself, your time, and your principles. Lo and behold, just like magic, you will automatically and unconsciously be more boundaried and assertive around those issues.

I call these endogenous boundaries. If you simply, spontaneously, and naturally value yourself or value a principle like freedom or truth or animals or whatever it is, you don't need to learn to have boundaries around that. You already do because you already value it. Your own morality, your own value system, is a shield, a boundary. It keeps you safe; it protects you. It means that if someone or some scenario is not aligned with your principles, your morality, or your values, then no matter what the advantage they offer and how happy the scenario makes you or how much pleasure there is there, you will simply leave.

You will know when you've hit a real boundary. In fact, it's quite easy to tell. You will know when there is real, decisive action taken on your part. For example, a real boundary would be asserted when you terminate a relationship with somebody, no matter what. If you keep letting a person get away with something because the sex is good or because they've promised to make you famous or because you're lonely or want some other payoff, then that is not a boundary. That's merely the fantasy of one we would like to have one day. Nor is that you showing yourself the real value of you, your time, or your attention.

So, how do we develop our own moral system of values in a world that, frankly speaking, couldn't care less about morality? Our culture seems to be doing all it can, every day, to corrupt morality.

Let me repeat. In my worldview, if you are moral and have a value system, you can still party, go out, drink, dance, and do whatever you want, as long as you have limits. If you come face-to-face with some beautiful, charismatic, wonderful person with whom you have amazing sex or they represent an amazing job opportunity and you find that they've done something that infringes on your value system, despite all the advantage of staying with them, you get rid of them. Then you have found a real boundary. You have found a true value, and you've found a morality. So how do we develop it? I will explain a method

I developed to help explore the creation of your own moral system in a later chapter.

The final demon that we must slay is the weakened and codependent sense of self. In order to differentiate NPD from mere arrogance, aggression, or bullying, the narcissist must exist inside of a fantasy. The narcissist must have and require a false self and a false sense of their place in the world in order to live in the world. They must see themselves through a grandiose lens in which they are all-powerful and worthy of worship.

Because of this false self, they treat mere mortals with contempt. People are not people to the narcissist. There is only one person to the narcissist: the narcissist themself. That is all there is, all there ever was, and all there ever can be. They have a false self, and it is extremely exploitative, aggressive, manipulative, and predatory. You will hear many people wrongly claim that narcissists are self-centred, selfish, and egotistical. Technically, this is false. There is no self. There isn't even actually an ego there at all. There is only superego. The ego itself is obliterated. There is only superego, impulsive id, and that false self.

Why is this relevant to codependence? Well, as a narcissist develops a false self, which is grandiose and predatory, we see them move into a certain type of story. You can think of it as a film they simultaneously write, direct, produce, and star in. The false self thinks of itself through a lens of delusion: it is the ultimate overlord, the ultimate predator, the smartest, the bravest, the sexiest, the richest, and so on and so forth.

But so does the codependent have a false self. The codependent also lives in a false narrative, which is that whilst the narcissist is the ultimate predator and overlord, the codependent is the weakest, meekest, smallest, and most agreeable creature on the face of God's green earth. Where the narcissist is bullying, codependents are submissive. Where the narcissist is demanding and creates scenes, codependents are giving and seek to restore peace everywhere. We codependents are martyrs, hoping that by being slavish enough we can avoid persecution. It becomes a kind of ideology that we really struggle to snap out of.

It's a false narrative, and we codependents must break free of it. We are not martyrs. We don't have to be the nicest people alive and give the best of ourselves to tyrants. We are just normal people, and we have rights too. Codependents have to internalise and live the idea that it is not honourable or spiritual to negate our own self for the benefit of others! We have our own dreams and desires just like everyone else, and we have the ordinary right to express those desires and pursue our goals.

The opposite of a narcissist is not a person with CPTSD. The opposite of a narcissist is not a codependent. Indeed, we know full well that narcissists have CPTSD. They are classic primary Fight, secondary Fawn responders on the CPTSD spectrum. This is how they try to control love. This is how they try to control attention. This is how they try to control the actions of the people around them: a cocktail of flattery and threats.

That's why a narcissist can be charming. That is why narcissists can be apologetic. That is why narcissists can pretend to care. That is why narcissists can be empathic. Because they don't just fight. They're not just aggressive bullies. If a grandiose narcissist is too much on the Fight spectrum, most likely a clinician would say this person is simply a psychopath. They have antisocial personality disorder or oppositional defiance disorder.

But that isn't the defining factor of a narcissist. They can also Fawn. They can also flatter. They can also draw you back in, to a greater or lesser degree, depending on the type of narcissistic personality disorder you're dealing with. They have CPTSD. So many will now say, "Yes, okay, perhaps the narcissist has CPTSD, but the narcissist is not a codependent. The codependent is the polar opposite of a narcissist."

Not so. Let me try putting it this way: if you are drawing your sense of self singularly from others, then you are, in my view, the definition of a codependent because you cannot be independent. If your entire value system, purpose, and mode of being in the world is dependent on the emotional reactions of others, then you are, in my view, a codependent. The people who understand psychoanalytic theory and psychotherapy will say, "Ah, yes, but there are counterdependents, and you could be interdependent." And so forth.

I like to keep it simple because I am, at heart, a simple being. Are you relying on other people to moderate your sense of self? Are you relying on other people to help you moderate your emotions, your life narrative, and your personality, such as it is or is not? Are you relying on other people? Do you depend on other people for internal activities and actions that should be done on your own? If yes, you are codependent. Narcissists and codependents are raised in very similar environments though not exactly the same. A narcissist must, at some point, be spoiled in order to develop the entitlement that they have. But both narcissists and codependents are raised in adverse childhood conditions. They both develop CPTSD and codependency. Whether codependent or narcissist codependent, they were most likely raised by highly narcissistic people who couldn't let them have their own space and their own boundaries. Why? If that parent were NPD, they may have experienced their child asking for space as a narcissistic injury.

There is another element to consider here, which is the controversial diagnosis most often given as "comorbid" (a second condition that exists alongside the first condition) with NPD. That is borderline personality disorder (BPD). BPD is identified as having a very strong terror of abandonment, a very unstable sense of self, and extremes of emotional ups and downs that one might try to regulate with alcohol, sex, and other damaging coping mechanisms.

I suspect that narcissism in a child is created by parents who are both BPD and NPD. This would mean that, yes, parents with BPD would have their abandonment anxiety triggered when a child starts to develop their own independence, authenticity, and boundaries. They hate it. They see it as a sign that the child will leave them. So they smash these boundaries down. The narcissistic parent sees these natural developments of assertiveness and the desire to explore the world as a threat to their grandiosity and a threat to their place in the dominance hierarchy, which is at the top, make no mistake. They also smash the child's boundaries down just to stop them from inflicting narcissistic injury. Both abusive parenting styles find it necessary to smash a child's boundaries: the BPD to avoid abandonment terror and the NPD to avoid narcissistic injury.

The codependent develops a false self with very similar architecture, in its essence, as that of the person with narcissistic personality disorder. The person with narcissistic personality disorder develops a false self. It's the ultimate predator. It's the alpha male. The ultimate queen. She is all-powerful. She is all-knowing. She is all-desirable sexually. He is wealthy. He is frightening. He is intimidating. He has material power in the world. Whatever. That's false. It's grandiose. It's a false self. If there's no false self there, and they're not living in a delusion, they do not qualify for a clinical diagnosis of NPD. If a person does not live inside of a maladaptive (meaning it harms the person carrying it) delusion of grandeur that is a misperception of reality, it is not NPD. The person may be psychopathic. They may be rigidly individualistic or schizoid or psychotic. They may be selfish or arrogant. But they do not have NPD without living in a delusional, broken-from-reality, imaginary state.

The classic codependent situation is very interesting. What happens with the codependent is that, when presented with similar threats in childhood, instead of deciding to descend into a fantasy of agency, power, and omnipotence, they go straight for the Fawn response. They will become Fawn-Freeze or Fawn-Flight. It's very unlikely that a true codependent would develop Fawn-Fight. They will predominantly be Fawners. What does that mean?

Where the narcissist sees a predator or stress, if they are a true narcissist, they will attack it first. They will become aggressive and offensive. They will find a way to harm the thing that has caused them pain. Yes, if they are a covert or fragile narcissist, this will only take place inside their own heads, but still, it happens. With the codependent, their instinct biologically at a survival level is to Fawn and supplicate, to find a compromise. In the face of a predator, they will want to give something away. The codependent is obsessed with giving parts of themself away to others. Money, time, attention, love, charisma even. Whatever it is, they become attached, trauma-bonded, and conditioned to give parts of themself away to people who are abusive and tyrannical. Just like they were forced to do in childhood, they're now unconsciously choosing to relive that trauma again in adulthood.

The codependent child is so attacked and so abused that they cannot find the strength and the determination to become narcissistic and grandiose, perhaps because their reality tests are too strong or perhaps because they have too great a sense of themself in the world. Perhaps they have too high a level of empathy, and they feel compassion for other people when they attack them and hurt them. Whatever it is, they can't do it.

So what we codependents do is develop a false self, the ultimate prey, the ultimate martyr, the most submissive, the kindest, the most agreeable, the gentlest, the most unharmable person. Why? Because we believe in our childish fantasy, which develops before the age of eight—that if we are kind, if we are good, if we are giving, if we are Fawning, if we give ourselves away, the predator will leave us alone. If it works and the abusive parent, the abusive teacher, or the abusive priest does leave us alone when we acquiesce, we are essentially trained to believe that the Fawn response is effective and the best way to handle life.

What happens then? We retreat from reality. We leave a false self, a scarecrow, an avatar, if you like, of the individual outside, visible to others, there to be attacked. And we ourselves withdraw into a cave. We leave the false self outside the cave.

You can bite it. You can attack it. You can eat it. Doesn't matter. It doesn't hurt us because we are good at dissociating, good at freezing, good at running away, and we're good at Fawning. Then what do we do? We withdraw farther back into the cave away from the stresses of the world.

Then what do we do? Well, we find that the stresses of the world and the threats of the world are getting into the cave. So we shrink. Then what? We've shrunk. We're in a cave. We're in the dark. But somehow the predators are still getting in. So we turn ourselves invisible. It doesn't work. The predators still come. We're still in distress. So what do we do? We become tiny, invisible, and we hide in a crack in the back of the cave. It's the only thing that works. Codependent people have an extremely weak self because eradicating themselves and their sense of self is a survival response to the predatory environment they were raised in. We cannot help but to self-eradicate.

What is the solution to this? It is not easy, my friend. If you've lived an entire life codependently in ultimate Fawn mode, totally agreeable, totally kind, never saying no, and always giving of yourself, you will find it very hard—very, very hard indeed—to do anything else. But you must. Without a self present, we are not living. Without a self present, we are not being honest. We are not being authentic. We are not telling the truth. Because we can't. Because we're not there. We don't know what we want. We don't know what our preferences are. We don't know what our morality or our value system is. That's why we tend to find very aggressive, tyrannical, abusive people to attach to so that we can absorb their value system, or junk value system, and that stops us from feeling numb and invisible and nonexistent.

A true codependent doesn't live. They haunt their own lives. They live as ghosts. They hang around. They're like kabuki actors at the back of a Japanese play, dressed in black, just there to help the actors, the narcissists, on the stage itself. We must be brave and strong and learn to summon ourselves back into reality.

CHAPTER 6

MALAYSIA: DEATH, REBIRTH

I HAD A VERY DIFFICULT TIME FOLLOWING MY BREAKUP WITH
Wu. Weeks turned into months. My condition was deteriorating. I was utterly heartbroken, and my emotional state swung from the depths of blackest depression to the hysterical, keen, electric television whine of all-out anxiety. I knew I was starting to lose my sense of self.

It was 2009, and I had already booked a holiday in Phuket, Thailand. It was my first time going to Asia. Though I didn't feel up to it, I decided getting away would help me. As it transpired, I ended up staying in Thailand for about three months before going to Kuala Lumpur.

These were not happy times for me. Though I was in a beautiful country, and I was working, everything came through a thick veil of grief, and my life was rendered joyless. I just couldn't figure out how or why I had ceased to be a fully functional human being. I knew something was wrong with me but couldn't figure out what. In retrospect, I would say that at the very least I had dramatically underestimated how bad my childhood had been and how wounded I was. I also realised that no one had ever bothered to train me in how to be an adult male. I was traumatised and totally unequipped for the journey into adulthood, but bereft of this knowledge, I simply did what everyone does: assumed I was defective and blamed myself for being a "loser."

One of my best friends from childhood, Raj, had by this stage moved to Kuala Lumpur for work, so I went from Thailand to stay with him for a few months. We had a few conversations about what I was up to, and, since I'd never held back on the slightly weirder view of life that I had, I told him I felt I had been cursed. Before the breakup, my ex's mother had confided in me that her daughter had used a love spell on me that involved putting her period blood in my rice in order to prevent me from leaving her. At the time, I wasn't sure if she was joking or not, but now the thought was feeding my paranoia.

As it happened, Raj knew a girl—we'll call her Saleha. She was a news anchor and a model, and her horseback archery trainer was also a Sufi healer, a gentleman called Pak Din. Raj introduced me to her, and after some negotiations back and forth, we agreed that I could meet with her trainer to see if he could help me.

In the sultry, damp jungle heat of the Malaysian capital, this story gets strange. I make no claims to the veracity of it and will simply report what happened to me. It will be natural to ask if I believe what happened as it happened, and to this day I'm still not sure.

We met in Nando's at the Mid Valley Mall. If you don't know Nando's, it's a Johannesburg chain that specialises in Portuguese-African style chicken called peri-peri. It was the least spiritual meeting place imaginable, but there you go.

Pak Din didn't speak great English. My Malay was limited to greetings, restaurant orders, and supermarket speak. So we largely spoke through Saleha, who speaks fluent Malay and English. Pak Din had various questions for me, and after thirty minutes of back and forth, he concluded, "This man's *semangat* is broken. I might be able to help him, but he must be tested first."

Semangat is a Malay word translating as will, intent, energy, passion, and vibe. You can say "*Semangat!*" to mean "keep going" or "cheer up" to someone struggling, or you can say that a song that energises you is a *semangat* track.

He was right. My *semangat* was broken.

Within a few days, I was to show up for my test. We went to the edge of a forest (Malaysian forests forever encroach on the city landscape, and you can hear monkeys playing and fighting within) that was by the horse track where Pak Din was working.

He handed me an old Malay bow and arrow. Not one of those fancy, weighted, light carbon fibre things. An old dusty Malay bow. He showed me a target and how to draw and fire. He hit it the first time and said, "Try."

I tried and failed to hit the target. I said, "I can't do it."

He said, "Keep trying make hit." Then I think he walked off, trusting me not to just walk up to the target and shove the arrow in it by hand.

Malaysia is a Muslim country, so walking around in a vest and shorts is not approved of, generally speaking. But also, like any hot country, status is withheld or given to those who cover themselves. I did not have cotton trousers; I had jeans. I had no lightweight shirt; I had an old Iron Maiden T-shirt on. Within no time at all, I was drenched in sweat.

The bow was an absolute bastard to draw, and pinching the arrow and fletching to take the shot put so much pressure on my thumb, the pad was totally numb for four days afterwards. But I kept going. I kept trying.

As Saleha had taught me, there is a hadith in which the Prophet tells his followers to "teach your children swimming, archery, and horseback riding." So the practise of horseback archery was seen as particularly Islamic.

Eventually, I got the old bow, my hand, and my eye to work together to coordinate a rather limp strike of the target. The arrowhead was pointing up and the fletching down when it struck, but it hit.

I called to Pak Din, and he came over and was pleased. He told me, somehow in his broken English, that "only bow and arrow can kill the demons; guns won't work." We were now to prepare to "fight the demons of the apocalypse."

In Islam, there are evil Djinn and Shayatin, and there is a time of tribulation and Armageddon that leads to a day of judgment.

But even as I had some vague understanding of this, I still laughed when Pak Din said it. He, however, did not.

He said, "I can train you."

I replied, "Great. When do we start?"

He said, "Tonight in your dreams."

As I drove home, I didn't know whether to laugh or cry. I'd come so, so far to have this last little bit of hope dangled in front of me, only to find it was the musing of a madman and a charlatan.

That was...until I fell asleep.

What followed were the types of crystal-clear visions I've only experienced with psychedelics.

Pak Din and what seemed like a group of other men, whom I could see spanning back generations, appeared to me, their forms echoing with ghostlike shadows of the men who came before. They wanted to know something. We went out into space, and amongst the stars I was asked about who my parents were. I was to show them the face of my mother and my father. The impression I got was that this group was going through records to check on my bloodline.

Then they wanted to know what was important to me, what I wanted my life to be about. They asked questions, but they really didn't offer me any dogma themselves. Did I believe in God? If I did, how did I conceptualise that? I would then show them a kind of moving vision-concept against a backdrop of stars, and they would say "Hhhmmm" and talk amongst themselves.

"Who do you think you are? And what do you think your purpose is?" And I would show them, and they would confer.

This went on for some time. My next impression was of being taken to a Malay jungle and shown an ancient spacecraft covered in Pali script. Then I was taken to a mountaintop where other spacecraft were being built and was shown around as though I was a new worker on the job. These visions repeated with some variations over the nights of the weeks that followed.

I began building and testing a craft. We would fly it over the land of an alternative world. A place where the geography is very, very different. These dreams are very functional, with an academic, sober, and engineering focus to them. I still get them occasionally to this day.

Just last week, I woke up in the middle of a dream that was effectively a lecture delivered from space looking down at the alternative world where I was being told, in a very calm and matter-of-fact way, that the movement of this particular weather system over this particular (nonexistent) island would affect the entire climate of the planet and how. Then I got a series of very high-level, virtual reality simulations of cloud formations, the way wind patterns shift, and so on.

At the Jungian level of metaphor, this could be understood as my life helping people with psychology. We build craft (new courses) to help people travel to "new worlds" (their potentiality), using ancient and modern technology (syncretism between ancient mystic and spiritual ideas of human potential and modern science). The weather systems could be moods or perceptions shifting.

One of the earliest recurring dreams, which I don't get anymore, sadly, was a really fun cinematic romp through the seven heavens, chasing down and blasting demons with celestial bows and arrows and magical spells that can be thrown from the mouth like a grenade. The colour and look of these dreams would be a non-Arab's interpretation of Arabic styles. Everything is arabesque. I am not alone; there are other warriors fighting alongside me. We are the Arabesque Avengers. In fact, the closest thing I've seen to these dreams was the 2012 Avengers fight against the Chitauri.

Perhaps we really are in a spiritual war against an evil alien army of demonic entities and can only fight them in our dreams. Perhaps, in a certain sense, we all are avenging heroes fighting back multiple evils in our daily lives, and this is the metaphor that manifests. I honestly don't know.

From then on, I knew that I had been accepted into something bigger than me. I knew that Pak Din, as promised, would pray for me and that if I did what I agreed to do—fight the demons of the apocalypse—I would continue to get stronger and better.

But I must be honest. It didn't switch overnight. It was a start, but the real legwork of the healing process was left to me.

I was invited to become Muslim and have been invited since. I'm regularly told that I am essentially Muslim, but I have read enough to know that I would fall at the first hurdle. Though

I don't think the modern Western scientific view is even remotely close to giving us a full picture of life, I could never sincerely state, "There is no God but Allah, and Mohammed is His messenger." I have too many questions that get in the way of the relief such a simple statement of faith would no doubt give me.

From this experience, I learned a lot about Islam, and I think that those teachings are embedded into what I do with my courses to this day.

All religions require a discipline and some kind of a sacrifice. All religions require us to adopt a worldview that is not the worldview of everyone else around us. Many religions require that we tell the truth to the best of our abilities. Many religions— and we can include Judaism, Christianity, and Islam in their number—are humble and fear God.

This makes sense to me. If God isn't at the top of everything, who is at the top of everything? It's not like the space magically remains empty. A neutral zone full of empty air. No, in the absence of a god, we place ourselves. When God is absent and we place ourselves in that space, we become bitter, irreverent, spiteful, arrogant, and pleasure-seeking.

I don't believe in a god, per se. But I know that neither I nor any other human causes all that is to be. I do not summon myself into being. There is nothing that I can control that causes me to continue to be. Nothing. If I just disintegrate, I could file a complaint with the manager, but I wouldn't exist to write the email.

And so this experience also taught me that there are more

things in heaven and earth than are "dreamt of in your philosophy, Horatio." Or, in other words, we aren't as clever—clever as our fragile little egos would like to believe.

I was raised Christian, chose Buddhism, but finally find myself alone. Sometimes it gives me something to remember what I studied in Malaysia at that time. Islam means to submit to God's will. All Muslims are "those who submit." To some scholars, this means that all that exists at the will of God is therefore Muslim. To these scholars, everyone is Muslim, even if they say they are not. A "kuffar," or nonbeliever, is one who has buried away from the light the truth (the Arabic etymological root of kuffar) that there is only one God and that they only exist by His will.

You cannot convert to Islam; you can only revert to Islam. This is a nice reframing, I think. You are already there. Already with God. Just stop pretending, stop hiding, and submit to the truth.

Perhaps you don't like Arabic words or feel a certain way about Islam. That's okay. I'm not preaching. I would just say that, in the end, if God is all there is, then we all submit to all that is because all that is, including this book and the brain ingesting its contents, is there by the will of that almighty being. If God is not all there is but some lesser entity, it is not God. If there is no God, then all this reality that we experience through time is just a spontaneous and random occurrence, and there is no will and no submission to said will.

But when I look at the single factor of complex order in the world, I struggle with the idea of absolute random chaos spontaneously coming together to create K-pop, vanilla pumpkin lattes, and Facebook algorithms. Yes, okay, things can and will spontaneously become "pretend ordered" for a short period of time in a chaotic realm. But to see the complexity not just sustained but growing suggests that there must be some order. Why doesn't it all just collapse and wash away like trillions of waves hitting a rock over one hundred thousand years? A peak of order and falling back down into foamy chaos. Is reality really hitting the lottery over and over again every second?

Perhaps you don't like the word *God*. That's fine. I have sympathy for that position. Perhaps "higher order being" or "principle of order" or some other more complex term might have some appeal. Ultimately, if you wrestle with defining it long enough, you will probably give up and just go back to saying God.

If there is a God, we exist only by the will of this God. It must be indivisible and in all things. We cannot escape, hide, or be separate because all that we are and all that is must be taking part within and because of God.

I'm not a preacher and my intellectual and emotional commitments to these notions are at variance with each other and change with the seasons. I know, however, that I am not the creator of myself or this world, and I am not prime causation.

I am more certain in a different but relevant assertion: we either accept reality just as it is or we suffer in a hellscape of denial.

That hellscape of denial, a trauma victim's necessary response to immediate suffering that becomes a terrible burden beyond the disaster zone, is what held me in its grip. I felt trapped in a malaise of misery in Kuala Lumpur. I needed God, mysticism, and some fresh narrative with me giving some purpose to my life in order to escape from the trap. I love Malaysia, but at that time, for me, it was a trap I desperately needed to escape.

Taking what I had learned and applying these teachings to myself, I realised I needed to take some pretty drastic action. Prayer and meditation would help, but I had the old adage "you cannot think your way out of a situation you acted your way into" tattooed across my soul. I've always instinctively felt that taking action was the best way to generate new realities. Consistent action over time with a well-defined series of goals delivered with discipline was, I knew, the key to getting me out of my oubliette.

This mysticism-based discipline of consistent action over time that I took up was the single biggest factor in moving my life forward in the last nine years.

CHAPTER 7

EXERCISES FROM AND FOR THE HEART

IT WAS A RAINY NIGHT IN KUALA LUMPUR. THERE ARE MANY rainy nights in that place. When you're living in a jungle environment with a jungle climate, it rains heavily and frequently. I had already been to the gym with my friends that night, and then after the gym, I spent what little money I had left eating the cheapest and healthiest meal I could in Kuala Lumpur, which was chicken tikka with rice. If you go to a local mamak, which is a place run by Muslim Indians, it will cost you anywhere between one pound and two. The places are loud, hot, and fast, but the food is good.

After eating, I went home in my little, old Proton car, a Malaysian make, which actually had cockroaches living inside it. It was filthy. There was no air-con, it stank, and it was always too hot.

When I got back, I wasn't ready to sleep, and I didn't want to do what I usually did, which was play *Grand Theft Auto* or *Call of Duty* for a couple of hours whilst listening to Jordan Peterson and Slavoj Žižek YouTube lectures. So I decided to take my notebook and sit downstairs at the bottom of the block of flats. I was living within the city suburbs in a place called the Happy Garden, which was a largely working-class Chinese area. There were very few white people living there, so I was something of an anomaly. I accepted that fact as well as the stares and oftentimes passive-aggressive, cold hostility that came with it.

At the bottom of my block of flats, there was an old, broken sofa. During the day, the aunties would congregate there and gossip and smoke, but at night, very few people were ever there, making it a quiet place for me to sit and write my notes. On this particular night, I know I must have sat there between 10:30 and 11:00 because around 11:00 p.m., the mass of Vietnamese hookers who lived in the apartment above me came down and got into the minivan that took them out for a night's work to the karaoke bar and the massage parlours about half a mile away from where we were living.

I knew at that moment that I wasn't happy. I knew at that moment I shouldn't have been in that particular place geographically or emotionally. I had already had the experience with the Sufi master, when he had told me my *semangat* was broken. This was perhaps two weeks later. The Sufi master had told me that he would pray for me and that I would get better, but I wasn't offered a timescale. I wasn't told to follow any particular discipline. I simply operated from instinct.

I knew I'd been given an opportunity. I didn't know what the opportunity was for, not fully, but I felt grateful. And I felt a sense of appreciation for having been given something, some small foothold. I also had a very strong sense that the expectation was for me to use that foothold alone. It was clear I would not be mollycoddled. I would not be given any more guidance. I'd been given the chance to dig my way out of the hole I was in. And I would either take it and, by doing so, prove myself or fail.

That night, when the Vietnamese hookers jumped into the van, chatting cheerfully and calling to each other, I watched them quietly, listening to the night sounds of the jungle just beyond the edge of the city limits. I had my notebook but no real intention of writing anything. I just liked to bring it with me. At some point, as I was thinking about the course of my fate, I asked myself: What is change? How does a person really change their life? I must've been around thirty-three or thirty-four at this time. I was single, desperately lonely, depressed, overweight, and had a life that really didn't make any sense. I didn't know it at the time, but I was actually quite mentally ill. I was suffering with some pretty extreme symptoms of CPTSD from the various incidents I'd been through in my life, but I really did not understand that at the time. I'd never really admitted the impact my sexual abuse and childhood experiences had on me, but the scars were large and deep. Some of these wounds had not even become scars. They were still open, and they were still weeping. I was ignorant to this fact. I knew that I was not happy. I knew that I needed to change, but I did not yet know *how* to change.

I'd consumed a tremendous amount of literature on personal development, magic, spirituality, psychology, and philosophy. So I started asking myself questions. The larger-than-life, all-American life coach and motivational speaker Anthony

Robbins likes to say, "The quality of the questions you ask determines the quality of the answers that you get." So I opened my notebook, and I wrote down the question, *What is change?*

Once I saw the question written there, a series of answers began to flow forward. I answered it not from my perspective but the way Anthony Robbins might answer it. I knew, from their work, that I had to define where I was and where I wanted to be with clarity and specificity and then bridge the gap between the two states as best I could.

I started to write in my notebook exactly where I was physically, emotionally, and financially. The finance part was stark and shocking. I wrote down how much money I was trying to live on per week. It was not a lot. It was far less than I had been earning three years before.

I wrote down where I saw my life going in the future. I wanted to know where I was, and I wanted to write it down explicitly. I also wanted to know where I wanted to be, and I knew that I would have to write it down for clarity, following in the tradition of the American New Thought movement and all of the motivational speakers who were its descendants.

I think it was Zig Ziglar who said, "It is hard to hit a target that you cannot see, but it is impossible to hit a target that you do not have." In neurolinguistic programming, a discipline I had been studying since the age of fifteen, part of the notion of "structural well-formedness" when setting a goal is to set it in positive terms and as clearly as possible.

So I wrote down where I wanted to be. I wrote down how much

money I wanted to be making weekly, how much money I wanted to be making monthly, whether I wanted to be in a relationship or not, where I wanted to be in terms of my health, what weight I wanted to be at, and how I wanted to be living my life.

When I was done, I looked at it all, and I took a breath.

I thought, *Is this realistic?* Yes, it seemed to be realistic. So I thought, *Okay, how do I get from where I am to where I want to be?* I knew that one of the principles of magic and one of the principles of old spiritual religious systems is discipline that forms a pattern of consistent action over time toward a stated goal. It's all in the daily and hourly habits of our lives. We think in terms of big herculean efforts and dramatic action, but really it's the little actions that build empires.

You see this reflected in martial arts practice. Martial arts tend to be a syncretic adaptation of psychology, philosophy, and magic. The Chinese word most often associated with martial arts is *kung fu*. The actual word for martial arts in Chinese is *wushu*. *Wushu* literally translates to "the art of war." *Kung fu*, more interestingly, translates to "hard work and skill developed through discipline." This means that you can have good kung fu as a chef, a dancer, a golfer, a writer, or at any skill that you develop over time that takes discipline and consistent action.

So I began to ask questions, good questions. *Knowing what I know about these things, what do I need to start doing in order to make real, lasting change and progress in my life now?*

Many of the core principles in arts like aikido and ninjutsu, which I had studied as a younger man, relate back to Buddhism.

One of the major goals of Buddhism is to have an absolutely crystal-clear perception of where you are and who you are, free from maya, free from illusion. So the first step I took was to write down certain things about my perception of myself. I think I did this maybe four or five times over four or five nights on the broken-down couch underneath the block of flats whilst listening to the rain and jungle birds and waving the bats away.

Specifically, I focused on how I saw myself versus how other people saw me. When I was in university, I was forced, very much against my will, to study accounting for the management part of my degree. I remember very, very little of it, but I remember how to write a profit and loss account. It's usually just two columns. I thought, *I'm going to do it like that.* So, in the column on the left, I wrote how I perceive myself, and in the column on the right, I did my very best, with compassion and empathy, to visualize how other people saw me. I did this exercise sincerely with the attitude of a person who is prepared to go deeply into the truth, no matter what they find or how much it hurts. The intention with which we do things like this is paramount. I wanted to know the truth. I was frightened of the truth, of course. I knew it would be ugly, but I tried to be as courageous as possible.

I'm not ashamed to tell you now that what I saw there really appalled me. The gap between who I thought I was and how other people must have seen me was huge. I had an idea of myself, largely speaking, as a kind, compassionate, warm human being. But when I looked at how other people must be seeing me, when I took it from their point of view, when I appreciated with compassion where they were coming from, I saw a very different picture.

Let me say this first: I think a lot of people who are dealing with issues around childhood trauma, CPTSD, and codependency really struggle to understand fully how other people see the world and how other people view them. We, the ones struggling with CPTSD and codependency, have a tendency to be extremely hypersensitive and hypersentimental, and are quick to feel hurt. We often seem not to fully appreciate the simple fact that most people, the normal people, simply do not have the time or the inclination to figure out who or what we really are beneath our surface act.

This is probably useful to remember: in the first five seconds that they put their eyes on you, people will often just take the first few cues that you give them about who you are, and they will run with that unless you do something quite dramatic to change it. It's not just me saying that. The psychological research on how we assess other human beings and how we judge them is clear. We predominantly do it visually, and we predominantly do it within the first five seconds of meeting someone. Why do we do this? Because we don't have time and because most people are not philosopher kings, world-class psychotherapists, or monks working to raise the consciousness of humanity as a whole. Why on earth would people offer you anything more than the bare minimum? They are busy with their own things.

Let's remember that it's not our job to see someone and try to figure out the depth of their trauma and the profundity of their soul. That's not our or other people's responsibility. The fact that many of us have this sense that it "should be" (in a just world) is an emotional hangover from a childhood in which we were not seen, we were not cared for or understood, and we were not raised in a kind or just environment.

In the adult world, it's good to remember that people have other things to take care of. We have bills to pay, relationships to hold together, and jobs to do. And all the other things that life throws at us. Don't be too hurt if people don't make a big effort to find out who you are and just take the superficial signals you have put out there. They are, after all, your signals.

I thought about this, and I thought, *Hmm, I think perhaps I've been angry.*

Looking back, of course I realise this is neither fair nor rational, but when we come from childhood trauma, our reasoning seldom has much to do with objective morality and more often to do with subjective pain.

I sat and looked at my notebook and thought to myself: I think I've been angry and disappointed with people because they couldn't see how much pain I was in. They just took the superficial signals I was putting out and made assumptions about me and essentially abandoned me.

But then, I reasoned, how willing have I been to see how much pain there is within other people? When have I looked beyond the surface for other people's pain? Sure, if I had a friend and we were close and they had a problem, I would happily listen to their problems for hours. But that's different. When was the last time any of us was really looking to see how much pain a stranger was in? And remember, to most people that I meet and to most human beings that you meet, you and I are strangers. There is no reason for them to see how much trouble you're in or to see how much pain you're in. And there is no reason for them to do anything about it as such. Nobody really owes you that, do they?

To people who haven't been raised in traumatic environments, what I'm saying probably sounds perfectly obvious and redundant. You might think you don't need to say this. You don't need to write this because people already know it. To those of us who were raised in adverse childhood environments though, this is something of a revelation because we are still stuck in our childhoods. We're still stuck, hoping that some adult will see our pain and rescue us from it. But if we are seeking to mature emotionally as adults, we must let go of that, and we must remember: childhood is over, and nobody is coming to save us.

As I said, I saw myself as warm, kind, and compassionate, but when I looked at how other people saw me, I realized that I was asking a lot from others. I was a hundred-kilogram, white male in a largely ethnic Chinese area, in a largely conservative, Muslim Southeast Asian country, with a shaved head, who dressed shabbily, who swore a lot, who was quite loud, and whose jokes were aggressive and frequently sexual/violent/politically incorrect and shocking. I realized that if I looked at myself objectively, came outside of my own solipsistic perspective, that if I met me with an understanding of the personality disorders, I would wonder if the person I was speaking to was all there. If I met myself at that time, I realized as I wrote in the journal, I would probably wonder if this person was some kind of psychopath, who was sort of a baseless, groundless, vagabond type drifting through the world very, very disconnected from reality and from the people around him. I also wondered if I wouldn't think of myself as having BPD as many of my behaviours were shocking and reaction-seeking. Hence the swearing, the vulgar sense of humour, and the tendency to say things that were somewhat shocking. I wanted to be noticed. I wanted to be seen. But at what cost? At what expense? Did people want to be around me, or was I bullying them or manipulating them into giving me attention?

When I say I was appalled, I mean I was appalled. I saw something very, very ugly that did not match my intention at all. This was a very hard moment for me. It took me a long time to adjust. I would say that even now, as I write this seven years later, I'm still adjusting. I still have to remind myself of how other people see me. Yes, these days, largely when I get feedback from people, presuming the feedback is honest, people's perception of me seems to be congruent with my intentions, my values, and who I actually am. But even so, it is something to be monitored as any tendencies and habits of the past will sometimes spill forth from the subconscious if I am not watchful. Because they're manifestations of shadow, we never know when we're falling back into these patterns, so it's something to be watched.

The effect of doing this exercise for me was that I managed to form much better relationships with the people around me. I managed to be much more empathetic and compassionate with people's responses to me and more aware of the upper limit of what they could tolerate conversationally. Previously, I'd been resentful of people's tendency to judge a book by its cover or their tendency toward prejudice or even racism. But when I saw it from their point of view, I saw less evil intent and more just a lack of time, will, knowledge, or information on their part. They just weren't educated in that. And it was cruel, I would say, and impatient of me to expect more from them than they could give.

I used to be a person who would say that they couldn't engage in small talk. I look back on that now, and I have to say, I cringe a little bit. What an incredibly arrogant position as though you or I are too good to discuss the minutiae of daily pedestrian life. What nonsense. We are not such mighty kings and queens. We are not nobility at all. We are not the lords of the earth; we're just people. And that's fine. There's no such thing as small talk. It doesn't exist. Eradicate the notion from your mind. There is the opportunity to share the details of the shared experience called life with another human being that translates as the message: *I see you. I know that you are there. I know that you are a human being just like me.* When you discuss the weather or football or politics with another person, it is not the content of what you're saying that has any meaning really. The meaning is that you are talking.

Small conversations that are superficial are very important as a way of touching and reassuring other people. Yes, of course it's petty, of course it doesn't matter, but the context not the content has the meaning. You are having the conversation. You are bothering to look into another person's eyes and speak words to them. You are alleviating them, potentially, of loneliness. You may be alleviating them from the sense of shame that they have to do a job that they don't want to do. And that's why you're talking to them because they're a cleaner or they're serving you coffee or they're bringing you a parcel or whatever it is, or you're doing the same for them. They are a person, and they hope, they dream, they hurt, they are fearful, they lie, they love. Just like me and just like you. Try to be kind.

This exercise made me more compassionate and much gentler in my interactions. Yes, even to ignorance. Yes, even to prejudice. Racism, prejudice, and ignorance exist in the world. Raging against it or being violent toward it does nothing except perhaps increase it. We have to find a way to understand the people who have no will to understand us. We must. We must go first. Again, this is a very Buddhist idea, that where you want others to go you must go there first. Do not demand that they go there in front of you like a king speaking to a peasant. Lead them as a fellow human being. And in your heart say, *I know that you don't see me properly. I know that your experience has led you to have this illusionary, messed-up view of the world, and that's okay. We can change that together. I can show you, perhaps, a different way of looking at things. And it would be an honour and a privilege to be given the opportunity to do so.* It takes courage and a lot of humility. I will take you through more useful exercises later in the book.

CHAPTER 8

DEPROGRAMMING FROM NARCISSISTIC ABUSE

WHETHER THE NARCISSIST IN YOUR LIFE IS A PARENT, A PART-ner, a boss, or whomever, the process of deprogramming the cult-style brainwashing of a narcissistically abusive relationship is broadly the same.

Firstly, we need to understand and break the illusion of the "bait." Narcissists use some kind of lure to get us to consent to the main part of the brainwashing, which is the "shared fantasy." In order to get you to wilfully suspend your disbelief and go along with their promises—which are never, objectively, likely to be rooted in reality—you must accept that you will never get the bait or lure they promised you. Make no mistake, these lures are powerful things. They have to be to get an otherwise rational person to join the narcissist in their delusional fictions.

With a parent, the bait would be parental love and acceptance. Who could resist that? Breaking the illusion of the bait would be to finally accept that they are never going to love you as they should or fulfil any kind of meaningful parental role in your life. Ever. This means giving up on the hope that you will have a mother or father as such.

With a boss, the bait would typically be career progress, fame, money, or the fulfilment of your childhood dreams. Breaking the bait would be accepting that no matter how vehemently or frequently they have promised you, they are either incapable (the narcissist, of course, exaggerates their power in any field) or unwilling to ever give you the thing you were hoping for. For them to actually fulfil the promise would be the end of their exploitative control over you. Why would they do that?

With a partner, the bait would typically be the fulfilment of your romantic pair bonding, intimacy, or sexual needs. Ever read on forums (or experienced firsthand) about "love bombing" or how wonderfully attuned a narcissist is to you—how compatible they are with you in the beginning? What about how amazing they are in bed? This is all bait. Once they have you on the hook and get you to buy into the "shared fantasy," these aspects of the relationship may dry up altogether. The only thing I personally found that remained was the sexual intensity, but that may have either been self-serving on the narcissist's part or a way of anaesthetising me from the reality.

Narcissism likely has the same etymological root as *narcotic*. *Narkos* means to numb and to induce sleep. Think of the ways these "baits" induce a pleasant, dreamlike state in which we are numb to the multiple red flags of bullying and exploitative behaviour. Like a spider who catches its prey in a web only to inject a numbing agent into the prey whilst binding it in more webbing to slowly consume the target at its own leisure.

Accept that you will feel very, very sad at losing the illusion of what you were promised. Accept that you will feel very, very remorseful at losing this promised scenario after having invested so much time, effort, and energy into it.

We fight like hell to avoid feelings of sadness, loss, and regret. If you can't accept and work with these uncomfortable feelings (using the techniques I describe in the next two chapters), you will fall into the psychological state of denial. The ego defence mechanism called denial is so powerful we can find ourselves sleepwalking back into a relationship we know is toxic, desperately (and in a childlike fashion) seeking the precious thing we thought we had lost.

You cannot "lose" something you never had. It will be hard, but try to remember this when deprogramming from the brainwashing.

Secondly, having accepted the bait—which is a kind of transaction we either consciously or unconsciously consent to—we have to accept the hook of guilt and shame should we seek to withdraw from said contract. The target will most likely simultaneously feel like they are being ungrateful, selfish, or even narcissistic themself if they try to pull this hook out. A part of us will feel like we are giving up too soon, abandoning a vulnerable, beloved person, or welching on a deal we have made. The mythology of making deals with devils is eerily reminiscent of this kind of unspoken contract.

Nobody wants to be a quitter or a loser. Nobody wants to lose out on the opportunity of a lifetime just because they didn't "work hard enough" or "sacrifice enough." As much as I love a strong work ethic, you must be very watchful that your work ethic or sense of honour doesn't get hijacked, forcing you to double down on a scenario that, by any objective measure, isn't going to lead to any good place.

Accept that you will feel guilt, shame, and even struggle with the idea that you are being excessively selfish, perhaps even narcissistic. These are natural parts of overcoming the narcissistic relationship.

Thirdly, you need to understand the concept of the "shared fantasy." This concept, identified by a psychoanalyst named Sander in 1989, is a necessary and healthy part of any functional relationship. We need a shared fantasy to be in a relationship. In many ways that's the nature of a relationship itself: shared goals, ideals, fears, and values. A direction and a narrative that tells us, reassuringly, who we are and what our relationship is about. Through the shared fantasy, we grieve our losses together, grieve the failings of the relationship together, build a present that makes sense, and move towards a future that, for all its necessary sacrifices, is mutually enticing.

The "narcissistic shared fantasy" was identified by Sam Vaknin, and he has spoken about it extensively in his YouTube videos. Building on Sanders's work, Vaknin has suggested that the narcissist unconsciously hijacks this natural phenomenon to their own ends.

Imagine two spacecraft out in space. In order to get access to each other in the void, they must build a bridge. That bridge, its size, length, how it attaches to the other craft, and where on the other craft it attaches are all elements of this "shared fantasy." This is how we access each other so we can experience togetherness and intimacy.

Now imagine a spacecraft full of evil alien life-forms—nanobots that can manifest as any shape, size, or colour based on their ability to scan a human target and decipher what that target needs to see and hear in order to evoke a particular emotional reaction.

The human, lost and alone on its craft, of course, thinks it has struck gold when it connects with the most beautiful, kind, benevolent form of alien life imaginable. Physically, mentally, and spiritually, it is perfection. The perfect match. The perfect life-form with which to form a mutually beneficial symbiotic relationship. The human opens all air locks and gives this wonderful alien being access to all its files, data, and blueprints. It offers up encyclopaedias worth of data to the benevolent being thinking it will be a saviour to humanity.

All the while, the alien hive mind of nanobots is skilfully flattering and seducing the poor isolated and lonely human into giving more and more. Every time the human gives, the nanobot rewards the human with narcissistic supply about how clever, sexy, or funny the human is.

"Narcissistic supply" was identified by Viennese psychoanalyst Otto Fenichel in 1938. It's the adulation that the narcissist requires as a kind of sustenance in order to feel alive. It's the poor replacement for the narcissist's inability to feel normal self-love and care.

Slowly the human target becomes addicted to these ego strokes and begins to see itself through the eyes of this godlike alien being. *Yes, it thinks, maybe I really am super smart! And sexy to boot!*

In this way, the narcissistic nanobot preys on human fragility and addicts the human target to narcissistic supply much in the way it is addicted to narcissistic supply itself.

What does this mean?

A kind of addictive third entity is created in the narcissistic abuse dyad (two people relating together is called a dyad), which has its own gravitational, irresistible force.

Once we have become invested in and addicted to the shared fantasy, we are forced to try to keep it alive. If and when it starts to die, through therapeutic intervention, healing, reading books on narcissistic abuse, or even just reducing contact with the narcissist, we will find ourselves becoming very distressed.

Why?

Because this airlocked bridge from my sci-fi scenario above is now stuck in our psychic body like a person in a coma has tubes stuck into their physical body that feed them necessary nutrients.

Pulling it out hurts, sure. But you are tough. You can stand temporary pain, especially when you can see that day three hurts less than day one, and you can observe the progress, however slow. You can console yourself by thinking, *Okay, this sucks, but I'm getting better. It will take time.*

But here's the rub: it's not the pulling it out that is the truly painful, dangerous part. It's that after you have disconnected and started to reduce contact, left the relationship, kicked the narcissist out of your house, or blocked their number, you feel the pain and slow hunger that the lack of nutrient supply will naturally cause.

Breaking the shared fantasy is therefore the hardest step. Forgive me one more unpleasant metaphor: you are like a heroin addict going cold turkey from the junk that's been in your veins.

You will not see or feel steady progress. In fact, you will feel that daily you are getting worse without them! Why? Because you are in withdrawal from the narcissistic supply they plugged you into. Life will seem duller, more irritating, and less interesting, and you will experience yourself as a duller version of yourself, too.

This will be the hardest test in your deprogramming journey.

Accept that you will feel like you are deflating and losing yourself. Accept that you will feel like an essential, core part of yourself has died. Accept also that these feelings are illusory, that they will pass with time, and that coming back from this type of attack is brutally challenging. It may be one of the hardest things you need to do in this lifetime in terms of a challenge to your sense of self.

Indeed, you may feel like you are losing yourself. A kind of small death is the inevitable result of choosing to walk away from the mutually created "child" or "project" of the shared fantasy.

Remember this was not real. Remember that you have been tricked into chasing a mirage and that the real death would be in wasting years of your life trying to prove that you were right and that the mirage was in fact a wonderful, thirst-quenching oasis in a desert of isolation and disappointment.

My final piece of advice is this: consider the state you were in when you first got into the relationship. Were you stable? Happy? Surrounded by good friends and living the type of life you wanted to?

What was true in my case, and in the case of many clients I've worked with, was that we were already in a vulnerable state. In a new country or city. In a new job. Trying to "make it work." Perhaps stretched a little thin, personally speaking. Or even recovering from a crisis. At that point, we found ourselves beginning a relationship with a boss or a partner who offered the deal of a lifetime, too good to turn down.

What I'm suggesting here is that if you wish to recover properly from this brainwashing and ensure this doesn't happen again, make sure you are living a good enough life. It doesn't have to be perfect, but your basic needs for stability, security, self-expression, contribution, and connection should be met. The best way to get out of the cult of one is to live the kind of life where it has no appeal whatsoever. Who can lure a person with a bait that the person already has authentic access to?

If you've just started or are about to start, take heart. The deprogramming process is hard; I won't lie. So seek the help of a professional who understands narcissistic relationships. Once you feel you have good rapport with them and can trust them, open up to them about the best and the worst elements of the relationship. A good therapist or counsellor can keep you on track as you ween yourself off the supply given through the false narrative of the shared fantasy.

Remember you are carrying a part of that narcissist's narrative inside your head. Not all your thoughts or impulses are truly your own during this time, so never act hastily or dramatically. Take your time. Write down the pros and cons of any decisions on a sheet of paper.

Ask yourself, *Does this look like the kind of decision I would normally make or does this have the mark of the narcissist on it?*

A part of your consciousness is colonised by the narcissist because of the powerful lure of the shared fantasy. You will be doing the cult leader's work for him or her at this point.

Only when, through disuse, the bridge between your two crafts has atrophied, rotted, and fallen off into space will you be truly free.

Do not try to go through this process alone.

CHAPTER 9

OUR KUNG FU

TAKE A PIECE OF PAPER AND DRAW A LINE DOWN THE MIDDLE.
On the left put "what my intentions, values, and objectives really are when I interact with people" and on the right put "how I suspect people may see and interpret my intentions." Do it four or five times on different days. Be as courageous and honest as you can. Be willing to learn and willing to change. This had a huge impact on me psychologically and emotionally.

The second exercise that I committed to doing daily as a discipline had much more material effect in the real world. This exercise, which I will describe to you now, is based on my understanding of the core principles of magic, religion, and spirituality. I knew perfectly well from studying these practises that I critically needed to change the content of what I was mentally focusing on. I knew perfectly well how negative and pessimistic my thinking had become. So I decided that five times a day I would connect repeatedly with what I did want more of in my life instead of ruminating over the past that was full of painful experiences that I did not want. As I lived in a

Muslim country, in a valley where there were four mosques, I would never be able to forget that it was time to do the exercise.

So five times a day, I would go through a list of things that I did want more of in my life. Usually, in my waking hours, I would be focused on all the things that I didn't want and all the things that were broken. So I would focus instead on what I did want, in thought, word, and deed.

In thought, I would visualize the things that I wanted to experience as though they were happening to me in that moment. I would stick to visualizing those things until my emotional and physiological state shifted. That meant I would have to visualize it passionately, subjectively, and as involved as possible, simulating the reality until I convinced myself that what I imagined was real.

In word, I would state in positive terms only that which I wanted. I would never say, "I do not want hatred. I do not want depression in my life." I would say, "I want to experience more love in my life. I want to experience more compassion in my life." You'll note here that I don't think the opposite of depression is happiness. I don't believe that. I do think the cure or antidote to depression, counterintuitively, lies in compassion. Remember, compassion is like the famous icon of Buddhism, the flaming sword that cuts through maya-illusion: double-edged. It cuts both ways. If you only have compassion for yourself and not for others, that is not compassion. That is selfishness masquerading as compassion. If you only have compassion for others but not for yourself, that's not compassion either. That is codependency masquerading as compassion. It's slippery, and it's very easy for our mentally unbalanced, traumatic responses to slip in through the back door when we are discussing issues related to spirituality. We must be careful.

In deed, I knew that I needed a physical ritual, like my Muslim brothers and sisters around me who were washing their hands and bowing to pray five times a day. Many times in my life I had seen the power of physical action, so I knew that there were physical actions I would need to take several times a day every day for these new neural pathways to be set. I chose to take certain positions physically. From chi gong, five times a day, along with a hand "mudra" (from Buddhist Hindu traditions, typically a gesture done with the hands) and this finger position that functioned like an NLP anchor for me that I had learned when studying Togakure-ryū ninjutsu as a teenager. This particular mudra relates to being determined, focused, and having power.

To try it yourself, place your hands together and interlock the fingers. Raise your forefingers on both hands and let them touch. Raise the clasped hands to your solar plexus with the joined forefingers pointing straight up.

Five times a day, I would do the chi gong exercise. Then I would put my fingers into the mudra of determination. I would visualize in my thoughts all the things that I wanted to experience as though I was subjectively experiencing them in that moment. I would control the words that were running in my mind, and I would control my inner dialogue so that I was focusing only in positive terms on the things that I wanted. I did that five times a day. I was supposed to do it for thirty days. I think I did it for twenty. By the time twenty days were up, my life had changed so dramatically that I actually forgot to do the final ten days. Don't you do this! If you set out to do something, do it to the end, even if you got the desired result early on. There is a Buddhist saying: "Better to never begin, once begun, better to finish." Don't stop; if you set the intent to go to the end, then go to the end. When I did this, I still had huge impulse control issues. Don't be like me. Be better than me.

KEY POINTS IN PRACTICE:

A couple of points here of note. When we engage in looking objectively at ourselves, this exercise is useful to the extent that it's not something that we normally do. We are seeking here to break unconscious patterns of behaviour and to set new ones, so the more we are outside of our comfort zones the better.

It's not a particularly useful exercise if it's already a commonplace daily habit, which I know, obviously, it isn't for most people. How can I say this with such confidence? Because there is nothing in our cultural conditioning that would lead us toward the habit of taking a long, objective look at ourselves. Without going off on a rant, it's obvious that one of the side effects of being immersed in consumer capitalist culture is that we are trained to think of ourselves largely in terms of that which is being consumed and that which is a preferential selection for us to enjoy. Everything that we consume and everything that we prefer, we consume and prefer subjectively.

Over time, if this is reinforced, let's say, hundreds of times a day, thousands of times a week, hundreds of thousands of times over months and years, then we're being led into subjectivity. We're seeing the world largely as things to be preferred, to be chosen, and to be consumed, and we become invisible to ourselves. I'm not saying that this wasn't true in other times and in other economic systems. The tendency towards solipsism as a cognitive bias has always been suffered by humans. What I'm saying is it's particularly bad now, so we have to make extra disciplined efforts. We, who would seek to heal and then perhaps create a better world, are in a constant fight against the tendency toward subjectivity and solipsism.

Nietzsche phrased it this way: "That is why I go into solitude—so as not to drink out of everybody's cistern. When I am among the many I live as the many do, and I do not think as I really think; after a time it always seems as though they want to banish me from myself and rob me of my soul—and I grow angry with everybody and fear everybody."

The exercise of "objectivity of the self" does that. It is both empowering to you and compassionate to the people around you, and it makes you better able to form meaningful connections with others because you become aware of the signals you are sending out to other human beings consciously and unconsciously. You become aware of the subjective impact the signals you send out are having on other people. There is a Buddhist level of compassion here in this exercise that can be attained. We can detach from the personalization of the effects we have on other people.

You don't need to take it personally. You are seen a certain way by people. They might be wrong, but that's what they're reading from you. It's just data. It's nothing more than a signal. They're really not responding to you at all. You are not as judged as you might think, so you are not as condemned as you may have supposed.

The more you penetrate that perspective, the more you can

attain the Buddhist level of compassion where you see your-self and other people with greater clarity. Whenever you see things with greater clarity, as they truly are, there's always a diminishment of stress, anxiety, and suffering.

The second exercise in which you control your thoughts, words, and deeds five times a day trains you largely at a meta-level to become aware of your agency in terms of directing your con-scious mind. In simpler terms, it allows you to control what programme is showing on the TV inside your mind.

Why is this important? Well, again, we are not trained or rewarded in this culture for controlling the content of our own consciousnesses. We don't live in a culture where prayer and meditation are so broadly practiced that there's a nightly prayer session after the news or the sports roundup or a morning med-itation session led by your president or your prime minister. These are not normalised, daily things. Or perhaps in your cul-ture they are? Let me know, please. I will come to you.

Why is this not normal? Again, I would point the finger (and I'm sorry if I sound like I'm wagging it) at consumerism. It doesn't benefit a consumer capitalist system to have people in control of the content of their own minds. In fact, it runs counter to the agenda of selling people on things that they don't need and manipulating people into wanting more and more things. If you're in some degree of control over the content of your consciousness and the emotional states that you're in through meditation, through prayer, or through visualization, you become less and less marketable.

It behoves all of us to engage in some discipline that controls the content and the focus of our conscious minds. It could be meditation. It could be prayer. It could be visualization. I don't mind. I'm not a zealot or a preacher, so I don't demand that people follow some rigid dogma. I would, however, passionately assert that it will help you if you follow some kind of discipline that allows you to focus the content of your conscious mind.

What I did, when I was going through my own process, was quite specific. I made sure that five times a day I focused on a list of things that I wanted and on some solutions and some practical steps to get to those things. I controlled the words I was using inside of my head, my inner dialogue. I altered my physiological state, which is extremely important because we are not a body and a mind. We are a body-mind, and if it's not impacting your body, it's highly unlikely to impact your mind in any meaningful way. If you do it for seven days, you will have achieved thirty-five microsessions of reconditioning your conscious and unconscious mind into focusing on the things that you do want for your life.

When I did the "thought, word, deed" exercise, there were a few rules I followed, and I'll share them with you now.

VISUALIZATION

Rule number one: Imagine the thing that you want to have happen in the first person, subjectively. Don't see it happening to you as though you're a second person, like you're watching yourself in a dream. See it occurring subjectively. You're in the picture; you're in the movie. You can reach out and touch, taste, hear, smell, and see everything that's going on in that scenario as though it's happening.

Rule number two: Imagine that it is happening now, not in the future. That is a classic mistake; don't make it. To the unconscious mind, there is only now. And it's the unconscious we are appealing to.

Rule number three: "The YES rule." Whatever you imagine, pretend that your unconscious mind is saying yes. It's saying yes, and it's echoing back exactly and only what you just said your stated intention was. If you're a single man and you say, "I want a girlfriend," and your unconscious mind echoes back, "Yes, you want a girlfriend," then what you would be creating more of in the future is *the want of girlfriends,* which is another way of saying *the lack of girlfriends.* You say you want money, and the unconscious mind says, "Yes, you want money," then you are accidentally creating lack. But if you say, "Yes, I am in a loving relationship with a beautiful human being that I am in love with," then the unconscious mind can say, "Yes, you are in a loving relationship with a beautiful human being that you're in love with."

Rule number four: This rule is emotionality. If your visualizations do not shift you emotionally and make you feel some sort of enthusiastic, excited buzz, they're probably not quite right for you. You're probably editing your desires and trying to make yourself something that you don't really want. This is your opportunity. It's your body. It's your brain. You can do whatever you want in this moment, so please be honest with yourself about the things you want. And when you've touched on those things, you will feel an emotional shift.

INNER DIALOGUE

Rule number one: Always express things in the positive. Say what you do want, not what you do not want, and follow the yes rule.

Rule number two: Speak to yourself kindly when you're doing the exercise because if you don't, the unconscious will reject it because it's aggressive and confrontational.

PHYSIOLOGY

Rule number one: Whatever physiological movement you choose, remember it must break your normal state.

Rule number two: It's a pattern interrupt, so make the movement unusual. It cannot be just rubbing your earlobe or tapping yourself on the shoulder. You're going to have to move a little bit. I would prefer it if you stood up. The bigger, the more dramatic, and the more nonhabitual the movement the better. If the movement you choose is something that you always do, like, I don't know, folding your arms or putting your hands behind your head, that's going to have less impact than if you jumped into a horse stance and started doing karate punches. Move your body differently.

It's conditioning, it's training, and it takes time and effort. It's not natural to you, so you do need to be disciplined and push outside of your comfort zone. You won't always enjoy it. Because it's unnatural and because you want to train to the point where it is a natural, spontaneous habit, it is possible that this could take a couple of months. In the big scheme of your life, that's nothing. Expect it to take about eight weeks. If you don't hit five times a day, don't beat yourself up over it. Just try to do it five times a day every day for a couple of weeks.

It will be difficult in the beginning, but, as the famous Japanese swordsman Miyamoto Musashi once remarked, everything is difficult in the beginning.

CHAPTER 10

FIGHTING THE DEMONS OF THE APOCALYPSE

IN THIS CHAPTER, I WILL IDENTIFY FIVE PSYCHOLOGICAL demons and offer some solutions.

DEMON #1: EMOTIONAL DYSREGULATION

People who have had their boundaries infringed upon in emotionally abusive relationships eventually end up with emotions that are up and down all the time. If you find that you struggle with emotions that are so disproportionately strong that going about your normal life is difficult, it's likely you are emotionally dysregulated.

I teach people to use a hand mnemonic because it's easy and convenient, and because you can do it in public without anyone feeling the need to call the cops. As you go through each of these five points, you tap one of the fingers on the hand you do not write with. The hand you write with will be the one to do the tapping.

The recommended timing for this is five times a day every day for at least thirty days. It will take you ninety seconds to complete at first, but after a week or so you will have it done inside of thirty seconds. Simply stop what you are doing and offer this a little piece of your time and your attention.

1. Tap your thumb and remind yourself, "I am me. I am not my emotional dysregulation, my mood swings, or the perceptions that come from them. I am me." We do this to draw a boundary between the self and the turbulent emotional states.

2. Tap your pointing finger and ask yourself, "What do I want to feel? What is my intent in this moment? What am I getting done right now?" We do this to remind ourselves that we want to feel good and focussed and confident and to remain committed to our intent. If you are at work, then work; if at the shop, then shop; if driving somewhere, just drive. Don't drift!

3. Tap your middle finger and say, "My emotions are messengers; they are welcome here, and I listen to them. I value and appreciate them. I know their intent is positive and that they want to protect me." We do this so that we don't have a relationship with our feelings built on animosity. We want to be literate, intelligent, and flexible.

4. Tap your ring finger and say, "I have a good relationship with myself. I recognise my needs, and I meet them. I engage in self-interested action for my highest good every day." We say this because we usually love ourselves the way we were loved by our parents or our partner. It's an unconscious instinct. If we are overcoming a narcissistically abusive relationship, then our style of self-love will likely be self-

abandoning and self-neglecting (reflecting the abandoning and neglecting style of love we experienced). We have to learn to start showing up for and taking care of ourselves.

5. Tap your little finger and say, "I am my own self. I am only responsible for the things I can control. Other people and their problems are entirely their problems. I detach from the impulse to solve other people's problems for them." We do this so that we continuously remind ourselves not to take on other people's problems as our own. Yes, it will be tempting to fall back into the old coping mechanism when facing stressful or ambiguous situations, but we must learn to give people's problems back to them. An adult must learn to deal with their own problems as an adult. Helping them avoid this is unhealthy and weakening for both of you.

DEMON #2: THE NUMBNESS INSIDE CREATED BY EMOTIONAL ILLITERACY

If you are stuck, fixated on a scenario that you can't move on from even though you've been grieving it for a long time, and/or you feel numb a lot, then it's likely you are dealing with the issue of emotional illiteracy. The proper term for this is alexithymia. It sounds heavy, but it isn't. It's common after a traumatic experience that our emotions shut down somewhat, but we really need them online in order to make good decisions and to heal and thrive in life. I've designed this exercise to help reconnect you with your emotions.

1. Go online and find an "emotion colour wheel"—you'll notice there are a ton of words there to describe emotions you don't usually use to describe yours.

2. Think of an event in your life that you found painful or challenging. Using the colour wheel, try to identify the specific emotion you feel about that event as accurately as possible.
3. Using a pen, draw three circles at the top of a piece of paper. Put three words that specifically describe your emotions into those three circles.
4. For each of these three emotions, try to identify greater depth by adding another three words that describe emotions to each one. What are three emotions you think you might be feeling behind the primary emotion?

When you look at the page, you should now have several more emotions than usual to describe what you are feeling.

So what?

When we are illiterate emotionally (when we do not have the words to describe what we are feeling), many of our actions seem strange and volatile. But when we are literate, we can see that our feelings and actions make a lot more sense.

Imagine, for example, you told yourself you simply felt "pissed off" or "mad as hell" about something your partner did but then later found yourself crying with intense sadness over the event. You might feel a little crazy, and you will learn nothing about yourself.

If, instead, you wrote that you were not just "pissed off" but that you felt "indignation" and behind that was "disappointment" and also feeling "ignored," then you might learn that:

- Your anger was a mask for a more vulnerable emotion: sadness and feeling abandoned. In that case, moving into deep sadness and crying would make you not crazy but hurt and seeking to heal.

- Your situation with your partner triggered unprocessed feelings from an earlier time when you felt this specific combination of anger and indignation but also the intense sadness of being abandoned and feeling let down by someone you trusted. You may spontaneously recover a memory: *Oh, that time my dad did such and such...* This is good data for you to know about yourself.

There is a third benefit. You can more effectively find conflict resolution with your partner if you aren't coming from defensiveness and anger. You can verbalise (which you can only do if you are more literate and have more words at your disposal) that, "When you spoke to me like this, it made me feel indignant, hurt, sad, and disappointed just like I did when I was six and my father did such and such a thing." It's far more likely that your partner will be open to hearing you and possibly changing their behaviour than they would just from hearing, "You pissed me off." That gives them no data, no compass, and no map to work from.

When doing this exercise, I would recommend you do it in the right spirit to avoid frustration and to get the most you can from it. This exercise can take what you have won in the hand mnemonic and make those wins permanent with zero backsliding. So the juice is definitely worth the squeeze.

Do you remember when you were a kid playing with crayons and drawing a house with the sun and your family outside the house? You were relaxed, daydreaming, and enjoying yourself.

This is the state I want you to aspire to: dreamlike, childlike, and curious.

You are, with this exercise, building a bridge between your unconscious and your conscious mind and seeking to make that bridge as strong as you can. See this as an exercise in exploration and discovery. You can't get it wrong. It's like divination through instinct and intuition.

DEMON #3: THE CHALLENGE OF THE TOXIC SUPEREGO/ PERSECUTORY "INNER CRITIC"

When you've experienced a traumatic and abusive relationship or environment, the multiple messages you received in that environment become internalised and play automatically in your brain as something called "introjects." Like a broken answering machine, they annoyingly play the worst messages you've ever been given, telling you you're not good enough, not competent, no one likes you, and so on. This is fixable. When these introjects are attacking you, this is referred to as an "inner critic."

Here we adopt a yin-yang approach. I learned this from Pete Walker. The yang approach is something Walker calls "angering." When being berated by the superego, presuming you recognise the inner critic when it starts up, you can angrily resist the inner critic and tell it, "No!" As Walker says, you must

> Intervene and psychoeducate [yourself] that this is the voice of the internalized child abuser (parent/teacher/bully/cleric). I then say something like: "You've been brainwashed into seeing yourself only in a negative light like [the abuser] did. Your healthy instinct of self-protection has been driven into

hibernation, and you can revive it by telling the critic...to shut up. Or you can imagine your adult self going back to the past and using your anger to shut them up (like some loving relative or other adult should have). You can do it quietly in your mind with force or out loud with volume if you won't be disturbing anyone. Cursing at them and inviting rage into your words can gradually help you to separate and disidentify from needlessly abusing yourself...from being as mean to yourself as they were. You cannot do this too often. In the beginning you may need to do it many, many times every day.

In the yin element to his approach, Walker talks about placing a nurturing and kind notice of the self where previously there had only been a persecutory and judgmental part that acted in hostility. Walker writes:

I shift into saying something that teaches [clients] to shift from thought-stopping the negative noticing of the critic and replacing it with positive noticing of the self: "When you've sufficiently angered, you can then shift into positively noticing yourself by connecting with the hurt, innocent child you were and by expressing compassion, unconditional love, and care for them." I help the client at this point to recognize and own their positive traits, accomplishments, and essential goodness and to reflect them to their child. With enough practice, this process often invokes the client's tears of empathy for themselves and allows them to grieve out the fear and shame they were so unfairly burdened with. In any given therapy, I may do a lot of this in the first year or two, until they start learning to instinctively feel pissed off when some minor imperfection spins them out into an excruciating flashback of self-attack...to express anger at those who installed their critic through constant negative noticing.

The yang angering differentiates us from the toxic superego and helps us to create a boundary between our authentic self and this wounded part. The yin nurturing allows us to train the superego to do its real job: offer us guidance and support.

DEMON #4: A WEAK MORAL PHILOSOPHY

I don't want to get into another rant about the state of our culture today, but suffice to say that, unlike all other periods we know of in human history, we do not generally prioritise having any kind of moral philosophy in this one. This simply means it's very hard for us to recognise what is right and wrong and almost impossible to set boundaries against that which we can recognise as wrong. Obviously, this makes us vulnerable to narcissistic abusive types, and it makes leaving that type of relationship very hard as we can never quite make a good "hard boundary" decision that enough is enough.

But don't be put off by the talk of morality and philosophy. I only want you to develop a systemic structure through which you can effectively judge the world and the people in it as being essentially "good for you" or "not good for you" and then have the moral fortitude to act in accordance with that assessment. In other words, if you are tempted to do something (or someone) which clearly has all the markings of short-term pleasure but long-term pain, you should be able to:

- Recognise this simple fact consciously and clearly.
- Act in accordance with your values and keep away from such people and situations.

How to develop a moral philosophy?

Well, I could tell you to go and read a bunch of books written by other people who developed their own systems of morality, but I don't think that's the best or the easiest way of getting this job done. I also don't want you consuming more content and other people's ideologies.

My suggestion is to take out a pen and a piece of paper. Every few days, attempt to answer some simple questions. It's not a test; you can't get it wrong. Just try it and explore what comes up.

What is good? How do you know? What is bad? How do you know that what you have said is bad is actually bad? How should a person live their life? What does a good life look like? What do I believe the purpose of life on Earth is? Do I believe there is one?

There are plenty of books you can get, articles you can read online, and videos you can watch on YouTube that can offer you some ways of answering these questions in a fun and entertaining way. But remember this: I'm not interested in the answers you come up with. There are no final answers, and everything you write will ultimately descend into dogma along a long enough timeline. That's just the way it is. This book, now written, will have dogmatic elements. That's okay.

The thing I'm interested in is that you wrestle with these questions. Through these grappling sessions, you will learn to think and reason in new ways and to develop new strengths and skills.

There are no correct answers. Some of the greatest minds in humanity have failed to give us definitive answers that satisfy everyone. But we all must face these questions at some point if our goal is to recover from whatever wounds we have experienced and to try to live well.

DEMON #5: THE ANNIHILATION OF THE SELF

In Ovid's tale of Narcissus and Echo discussed earlier, it is worth noting that before Echo falls in love with Narcissus she is already cursed. Echo was a beautiful wood nymph who was very talkative and had a great singing voice. Zeus was fond of frolicking with wood nymphs, and when his wife Juno turned up in the woods to see where he was, Echo kept her busy by chatting away with her to distract her so that Zeus could escape. Furious at this deceit, Juno cursed Echo by stealing her voice and condemning her to only be able to repeat the last few words someone else had said. Hence echo.

In Taoist terms, narcissism is locked into yang. It can only transmit and never receive. It is the worst expression of masculinity: tyrannical, insistent, obsessive, and self-aggrandising. And echo is locked into yin. It can only receive and echo and never transmit. It becomes the worst expression of femininity: passive, indecisive, flighty, and boundaryless.

Echo codependents have no voice of their own. They have to find a tyrant to attach to in order to "find a voice" and to experience purpose vicariously. Even if that purpose is destructive to themselves. Echoes typically take place in empty spaces like caves. As you will see when I go further into describing this issue of annihilating the self, this metaphor becomes more significant.

When our sense of self has been so weakened by trauma and abuse that we do not dare to be, we are in what I would consider to be a fully codependent state. We need to be told by others what to do, what to want, what to think, and even **how** to want. Under such circumstances, we would typically choose people who like telling others what to do, be, and think. People who have this tendency are often quite psychopathic, narcissistic, demanding, controlling, bullying, and tyrannical. As a client in coaching once said to me, "It's not comfortable, but at least it feels like home."

If we are raised in or have in adulthood spent many years in abusive environments, this kind of self-annihilating (as in destructive of the "self") abuse becomes hypernormalised to the point that we cannot bear normal, healthy, boundary-respecting relationships. Our value system is now inverted. That which is safe and sane feels creepy and unpleasant, and that which is totalitarian and abusive feels like home.

As I wrote in an earlier chapter, just like the NPD, codependents create a false self, a scarecrow avatar of ourselves that stands outside our cave of isolation to be devoured by predators. We never really fully invest in anything with our authentic selves because anything and everything we ever authentically invested in was torn to shreds by predators. We come to expect this. It could even be argued that we come to demand it.

We might even be in a sacrificial cycle. Needing at regular intervals to exorcise the suppressed desires and emotions that inevitably are pent up by being dishonest and evasive about what we really want with a festival of butchery. It would have a ceremonial catharsis to it. A sense that the sins heaped upon us as scapegoats would be purged in the sacrifice of our effigy. We would, in this hypothetical scenario, need the abuse and the catastrophe it brings in a cyclical, repetitive compulsion to feel some relief from all the guilt and shame. We would be a party to our own scapegoating and abuse, in effect.

How to stop this? How to defeat this fifth and final demon?

The short answer is: I don't know.

I myself haven't done it. The process of my recovery from CPTSD and codependency is ongoing. Sometimes I've had help, guidelines, and maps. Sometimes, whilst stumbling in the dark, I've had to create my own solutions ad hoc.

One thing I can say with some confidence is that there must be some merit in strengthening the sense of self. This is an endeavour that takes tremendous bravery, and I think it's important to say that first. It will be uncomfortable and frightening and will take great courage.

Why?

Because there are many dark advantages to remaining in the state of "not being." I don't want to get sidetracked into a long treatise on why humans need and love to absolve themselves of responsibility, but suffice to say that we do. We will pay almost any price to not be the person responsible for the misfortunes of our own lives. We will pay almost any price to turn away from the dread of being a fully potent agent within our own life trajectory.

Are all people who abrogate responsibility fully fledged code-pendents? No. I would say that, much like the fact that many people who learn to behave narcissistically are not clinically diagnosable with NPD, the overwhelming majority of humanity is on the spectrum for codepedency but is not what I would consider a full, cave-dwelling, self-annihilated codependent.

Do people lie about what they want? Do they put on a false show to fit in? Do they cling to ideologies, public figures, and political parties that do for them (however indirectly and unfulfilling this may be) what they lack the courage to do for themselves? If the answer is yes—and I believe it is—then are many people walking around with lopsided smiles? Full of grief and frustration and pent-up rage? Weighed down by the burdens of missed opportunities and guilt?

Yes.

The real pandemic is not one of narcissism and psychopathy. The real pandemic (pan = all, demos = people, so a pandemic must affect the majority of the population) is, in fact, codependency.

How do we summon our self back from wherever it is hiding?

With courage, we need to relearn, now that we are adults and seeking to be sovereign agents in our own lives, that the better and safer mode of being is NOT in hiding what we want and who we are, but in telling the truth of it and being exposed to whatever the consequences of that may be.

Here we should call out the double bind we are in. We need to be courageous enough to be who we truly are and strong enough to deal with the consequences of that, but we've spent our whole lives hiding our true selves away and only presenting a false self so that if we are devastated or "eaten alive," it's only the effigy that takes the pain, allowing us to rise again.

How can a person who has lived cramped and invisible in the dark suddenly be ready to be strong and exposed and vulnerable in the light?

They cannot.

The only way forward is through small, consistent steps, and it will be no small task. We are set to undo years and years of unconscious conditioning to hide ourselves and our wants. Most of us have done this since we were born. We are conditioned to think safety and invisibility are the same thing.

We must learn to be visible. Yes, it will be more dangerous! The fear that being honest, open, and visible is riskier is not born of delusion, trauma, or neurosis. It's an accurate assessment of the situation we find ourselves in.

Okay, this is not such good news, but let's look at the alternative.

You keep living as you have: self-negating, invisible, a slave, your true desires hidden away in the dark, just an echo of someone else's desires. Slowly, over time, your will to be will atrophy. Your lust, your drive, your passion, and your health will go with it. If you are merely a ghost haunting your own life as a bit player, what would you need those attributes for anyway? Biology is economically miserly: if you aren't using it, the privileges of its use will be withdrawn simply to save energy. Have you ever been injured badly enough to watch with utter horror how rapidly your body atrophies? So it is with your mind and your spirit.

Are you unhappy with the way the last ten years went? The way the last year went? What if I told you I can 100 percent guarantee the next year and the next decade will look exactly the same unless you start doing major work to call yourself back into being?

I can't say that, of course. I'm asking you, "What if?"

Isn't it a bit like the old spiritual and magical ideas of the spirit being knocked out of the body whilst being possessed by another spirit? How do we magically summon that self back into the body? What if the self, correctly (based on all the data it has from prior experience) thinks there is nothing but pain and risk in the body being back in life, back in reality? Don't we then have the rather odd job of trying to convince the self that actually life might be better if we lived as a real, honest, vulnerable human being who inhabited our own lives? Of trying to convince the self that actually we aren't really "living" at all right now? That we are merely surviving day to day to do it all again tomorrow? How horrifying! What utter, wretched slavery!

Can we convince our selves that the only way back to life and living is through the courageous and authentic habitation of our own bodies and our own lives? My suggestion—and these are just suggestions—is to consider the following. Perhaps journal about them or discuss them with a therapist or coach.

Can I recognise the situation or persons with whom I'm triggered into a pronounced Fawn response? With whom or when am I at my most codependent?

Whilst I am here safely journaling or talking to my trusted therapist, can I consider other ways I could respond in these situations so that I can put my needs and authentic self forward in a way that allows me to be truly honest about who I am and what I want?

What would that look like?

At this point, I would like to apologise that I can't be more prescriptive. I wish I could give you the technique that allowed you (and me) to simply follow these simple five steps for seventy-five days and then everything would be okay. But no such thing exists. The reason is that we have lived a lifetime like this. Laying down new neural pathways is not going to happen overnight. It can't be "thought" into being either. We have to actually "act it out" in order to believe that this is a better way of being. We have to create new "reference experiences," which are memories of times when we showed up for ourselves and others as our authentic self and it was superior to hiding, self-abdicating, and Fawning to get what we wanted. From those reference experiences, the brain and the unconscious can begin to say, "Hang on. Maybe this really IS a better way of being in the world."

More questions to consider:

In what ways have I learned to hide who I am and what I want? Do these have elements that look like coping strategies or self-soothing techniques? Do I have destructive patterns of behaviour like addictions or bad relationships that allow me to hide?

What is the benefit of hiding? (Be sincere! Many bad patterns of behaviour stay in place because they "work" to a certain extent and are still advantageous; let's explore that.)

What would the benefit be in ceasing to hide and in having the courage to be?

And finally:

In what ways do I feel really safe just staying in my current lifestyle? In what ways would I be in danger living authentically and being who I truly am and expressing what I truly want?

Leaving behind codependency is like leaving behind a coping mechanism, an addiction, a false persona, and an abusive relationship all in one go. No one can or should expect it to be easy. But I believe it is possible. Even though I have not fully achieved it myself.

When I left Malaysia and moved to Spain, I very quickly found myself in the slipstream of another helter-skelter relationship. The details are not too important, but we found ourselves in the Balrog–Gandalf tumble within a month of moving in with each other. I knew very early on that she was sick and that she needed therapy rather than a boyfriend. But, to my shame, I stayed.

I stayed because she was beautiful and impressed my friends.

I stayed because my mum liked her, and I didn't want to disappoint her. I stayed because the sex was good. I stayed because I found being single and dating a painful and humiliating experience. I stayed and took the unjustifiable abuse, lying, and manipulation for three years because I am a codependent, and being bullied by the one person I have offered my love and trust to feels like home to me.

It goes without saying that this experience was extremely painful. Being with her was traumatic, and within about six months, I started to develop physical symptoms that reflected my stress. Not being with her was even more painful, so I kept going back despite trying to escape. Eventually she demanded I go to therapy because I was "sick, evil, wrong, and a *bad object*." So I did. In demanding this, she completely shot herself in the foot.

There are a couple of things to say about therapy and counselling that are of note. Yes, there are horror stories. You may even have some of your own. But don't give up on finding a good therapist whom you can trust and develop a relationship with. The therapeutic process, when with a good counsellor, is priceless in your recovery process as long as you are open and prepared to tell the truth and do the work.

What going into therapy in the midst of an abusive relationship did for me was broadly twofold. First, it introduced another adult mind into the midst of an insane, codependent reality tunnel befuddled by lies, manipulation, and gaslighting. In the dim light of a small Dublin counselling office, I found myself laughing with relief as I recounted the multiple psychological tortures imposed on me. In the sober light of day, with a good-humoured, sincere, and qualified human being listening to me without an agenda, the insane, demonic bondage seemed trite and almost comical. Having the light of another person's point of view shine into that darkness is very powerful. Don't underestimate it or be too cynical of the therapeutic process.

The second element that I found so helpful when speaking to this counsellor was his ability to challenge me. Jung spoke often of the "shadow." It's an unfortunately mystical-sounding term that evokes imagery. Unfortunate because the reality of our shadow is not that mysterious but perfectly ordinary and pedestrian. There are things about us, our beliefs, and our patterns of behaviour that are simply "not in the light," which means only that we cannot see them.

Over time, we run along with our map of reality and our ideas and assumptions of what is happening, and we make our decisions and then take action based on that map. What if it's wrong? What if we run for a long time in the wrong direction using a bad map and false beliefs?

We need to have our views challenged. Especially if we are traumatised, trapped, or in pain. The extreme emotional ups and downs we experience when in these situations are able to warp our perceptions. In Jungian terms, it's sometimes called "shadow activation." In Buddhist terms, we would have sunk into "maya." This simply means that we are no longer seeing reality as it really is but as our traumatised selves see it. When we view things through the lens of hurt and abandonment, of course the reality tunnel grows darker.

The challenge we face is to deliberately choose courage and light even though we have no prior experience to indicate that doing so will be of any benefit or use to us. When we look at the challenge in this way, it develops a kind of spiritual element to it.

Sometimes I ask myself: what if my experiences in Malaysia had a literal truth to them, at least in some dimension? Would that mean that there are people who have taken up the sword or bow in a spiritual war against evil? That there are actual warriors for truth, for light, and for love who want to push back the forces of trauma, deception, and lying?

Or is it really all just the metaphorical interpretation of a confusing and painful experience in the mind of a middle-aged man? Don't we all want to be special? Chosen? Heroic?

At this point, I think it's reasonable to ask: does it matter?

There is some metaphorical truth in this for sure. If we enter the narrative that this is a spiritual war—that the thing we are fighting for is nothing less than the human spirit itself—does that empower or disempower you?

Nobody wants to be that delusional nerd sat in a room doing little but dreaming grandiose fantasies of courage and victory, of course. I know that. But isn't there at least a shred of truth to this view of the situation we face?

You can choose the dominant ideology: consume and be materialistic. You are born, you live, you fuck, you eat, you die, they dispose of you (your flesh suit) in a nice little ceremony in as hygienic a way as they can, and that's it. Game over.

Or you can choose a different worldview. That you have meaning. That the bird that flies past the window has its own meaning. That there is a purpose and an order to this world, but that it is fighting against chaos and purposelessness. That this fight is not just "out there." In fact, most of the fight is to take place within our hearts.

This is the true meaning of jihad, the internal battle of good versus evil. If we, as individuals and as a collective, can face this battle, can commit to telling the truth and trying to develop a way of being in this world that is at least somewhat moral and virtuous (nobody is saying we need to leave the world and live as monks and nuns!), then I think we have a good chance of building a better world.

I think it's entirely possible to see the cycles of intergenerational, historical, and cultural trauma stopped. When I say stopped, I mean stopped completely. We simply don't need to hand this pain on. It actually takes more effort and burns more calories to be cruel than it does to be kind. When we are cruel, it burdens us. We know, deep in our hearts, that everyone around us is a part of us. We know, deep down, that everything around us is a part of who we are. We know, in the secret whispers of the deepest places of our hearts, that when we exploit or use another person, when we lie or steal from them, we are actually hurting a part of our selves.

When I went to counselling in Dublin, I was told by my then-partner to go because I had something deeply wrong with me. I found that I had the chance to invite another adult into a crazy little claustrophobic world created by two wounded people in a lot of pain and a lot of fear. I also found that I could be challenged in my assumptions and beliefs, which, as I said, was incredibly beneficial for me.

But it also did something else. Something much more important. It provided me with a neutral space in which I could explore and expand my self. When I'm using the term "self" here, I am thinking of the model in which the authentic self withdraws into the cave, then shrinks, then makes itself invisible, then hides in a crack in the back of the cave, leaving only the effigy "straw man" at the mouth of the cave, hoping that predators will devour only that and be satiated.

The focus on, prioritisation of, and expansion of the self is key to overcoming codependency as I have defined it: a lifelong tendency to annihilate the self in service of an "other."

To many, this will sound like a dangerously narcissistic endeavour. I would just like to remind anyone reading that "healthy narcissism" is absolutely key to the proper functioning of a sane person's ego. You *should* be self-serving and self-interested but not at the expense of others.

This is yet another enormously tough challenge for the lifelong codependent. We suffered at the hands of people who were self-focused and self-serving in a boundaryless and toxic way. We tend to be conscientious and driven by guilt, so will the prospect of mirroring such abhorrent behaviour and possibly hurting others be appealing?

No, it will probably create a sense of revulsion in the lifelong codependent. Yet, as with ancient folkloric medicinal practises where the thing that stings you usually has the thing that will heal you growing nearby it, so we must explore the idea that even though it was narcissism that wounded us, it might be precisely a dose of (healthy) narcissism that saves us.

Here I speak as somewhat of a hypocrite. I have not, myself, internalised the notion of "healthy narcissism" or self-interested action to any meaningful degree. Even though I realised a few years ago that it was necessary.

Why not, you may ask. You are the doctor. There is the cure that you advocate. Why not simply take it and be done?

I would reply: for the same reason you won't. It's frightening, uncomfortable, and all the way outside of my comfort zone!

To be clear: am I advocating narcissism as a healthy way of life? Absolutely not. Narcissism is abuse and exploitation; don't do it. But IF you are a lifelong codependent who can only think in terms of the demands and drives of others as a servant to their will, then the only realistic cure to that would be to take that focus on the demands and drives of the other and place it firmly back upon the self.

When I did my counselling in Dublin with a perfectly pleasant, warm, and kind gentleman at the behest of an ex-girlfriend who was, at the very least, struggling with PTSD and a strongly activated outer critic, I found myself in a space (for one hour, once a week) where the only thing that mattered was me. And my feelings. And my wants. And my fears.

I noticed the invigorating effect this had on me. Where previously I had been anaemic and fragile in the assertion of my wants, drives, fears, and boundaries, I found myself becoming calm, decisive, and assertive. My ex's rants, taunts, and provocations no longer induced anxiety and rage but, rather, sadness in me. You might think, *Sadness? That's hardly an empowered state*, but I would beg to differ.

When there is anxiety and rage, there is motivation to control, make changes, take action, assist, or resolve. But in sadness, there is acceptance and the seeds of letting go of a situation that we finally come to know is not of our making nor within the boundaries of our control.

Sadness and grief are often seen as "weaker" feelings, but I would claim that there is no authentic growth or change without sadness and the grieving process that follows, which ultimately leads to acceptance.

Inside of a toxic relationship, the codependent will feel utterly compelled to fix, to parent, and to heal their partner, not realising that this is both beyond their responsibility and beyond their power. If you aren't in control of a person or a situation, how can you be responsible for it?

My ex, when she saw me switch from anxiety, Fawning, begging, or raging at her provocations to simply sitting in quiet, sad acceptance of her provocations, really began to panic. She instinctively knew that this heralded a major change in my perception of her and the relationship and that it would lead to me finding the clarity and courage to leave.

In my view, it's not so much that codependents lack the strength to leave; it's that they don't see the situation with enough clarity to realise that it simply isn't worth their time to attempt to resolve it.

Similarly, when people ask me about learning to be more self-assertive, I no longer assume that it's a lack of resolve on their part that's stopping them, but that they can't perceive that which needs protecting with enough value to bother protecting it.

I hope the comparison makes sense. If you truly value your love and your time, you won't need training in protecting it and asserting boundaries around it. You would just protect and assert. Instinctively and automatically.

If you truly have accepted that the person you are with is sick in a way that makes it impossible to continue a relationship with them, why would you need "strength" or "resolve" to leave? You would just see it for what it is, feel sad, and leave.

What I am driving at here is that people are not as crazy or "messed up" as they judge themselves to be. Actually, their decisions and actions make perfect sense based on their perceptions in that moment. When they see things clearly, free from gaslighting and provocation, the course of action becomes both obvious and easy—not pain free. You will be sad. You will need to grieve. But would you rather embrace sadness and grieving for what was not there and move on or remain trapped in an illusion for decades?

What happened to me? Over the course of my life, I've made a sincere (and, let's be honest, neurotic) effort to fit in. To give other people what they wanted. To do what society said I should do. I have given, in truth, an awful lot of myself away. In time, attention, money, emotion, love, energy, and everything else. Why did I give it? Did I give it willingly? Had you asked me, I would have said, "Yes, of course. These are my choices. I am awake and aware, and this is what I want. I like to help people. I like to be of assistance."

But the sad reality that I am slowly waking up to, through a thick veil of denial, is that I did not do this of my own volition. That in many senses, due to my experiences in life, I do not own a volition of my own as such. I have the semblance of agency and volition, but I am, in fact, a lifelong slave looking for a new master. Now, to be clear, it might not only be romantic relationships in which lifelong codependents find a master. It might be a job, a boss, a politician, an ideology, work, study, or something else. In order to attach to someone or something codependently, it probably will be exploitative, unfair, demanding, confusing, incongruent, and anxiety-inducing.

Ultimately, the codependent will collapse into bitterness after overgiving, hoping that their giving would be reciprocated at a 90 to 10 percent ratio (in which the codependent gives 90 and gets 10). In fact, they are giving 200 percent, carrying someone else's or something else's burden and getting nothing in return. Or less than nothing in return: insults, burdens, criminal charges, and so on. In the end, it may actually be expensive to be in these kinds of exchanges.

What can we do about this?

We need to be humble and to understand that we are part of a system that ends up being abusive. Yes, your online YouTube gurus will tell you all the ways in which your narcissist lied, robbed, cheated, and stole from you, but in the end aren't you actually only capable of controlling one person in the dynamic?

And isn't that person you?

What did you do?

If you let a person trample your boundaries, treat you like trash, cheat on you, and so on and didn't leave them, I don't want you to feel bad. Feeling guilty or ashamed is not going to help you one bit right now. But I do want you to see it clearly and to develop an understanding for what has happened.

No, it's not your fault. You neither consented to nor did you choose this—not in childhood and not in adulthood.

But were there things you could have done to protect yourself that you didn't? Were there warning signs you ignored?

Perhaps you should be looking to have a conversation with a therapist or counsellor about why that happened. As I said earlier, if you value a thing (the thing could be you, your love, your time, your kindness), then you will automatically defend it and set boundaries around it. Did you not do that? Then can we explore the possibility, nonjudgmentally, that perhaps for some reason you don't value yourself, your love, or your time? And if not, why not? And can we do something to fix that?

I know it sounds trite, but what I learned through all my experiences is really that we must relearn to value the self. Not with narcissism, but with humility and respect, and reverence.

Not because you (or I) are the centre of the universe but because you are a part of the amazing complexity of all that is. What a wonder! Your localised, individualised consciousness is totally unique. Everything you experience and have experienced and will experience in the future will be once and never again.

It's a bittersweet thought. We are so fragile. Life is so short. The world is so beautiful, in its way. And we have so much to be grateful for. Perhaps one of the first steps toward overcoming our trauma and codependency is to put down the smartphone and step outside. Consider the wonder of a bee or a leaf or a star. We didn't and couldn't make these things. When I think these thoughts, I become full of wonder at all that is and all that could be. The mystery of the world fills me up.

I'm not going to tell you that you need to follow a religious dogma in order to recover or that there is a spiritual answer. But perhaps we would all benefit from exploring and developing our own religion, philosophy, or spiritual view and from going into our own unique, individual, mystical practise to connect again with the infinite—in gratitude and appreciation for all that is.

I sincerely hope that this book was of use for you. Thank you for offering the time and attention to read it, and I wish you all the very best in your individual journey.

Printed in Great Britain
by Amazon

29559965R00101